CREDIBILITY

Nigerian Refugee Claims in Canada

CHARLES MWEWA

Published by:
ACP
Ottawa, ON Canada
www.acpress.ca
www.springopus.com
info@acpress.ca

DEDICATION

For

Gloria Ifedayo

CONTENTS

LIST OF CASES

Abawaji, Abdulwahid Haji Hassen v. M.C.I. (F.C., no. IMM-6276-05)

Abdi Ahmed, Ilham v. M.C.I. (F.C., no. IMM-3178-12)

Abubakar, Fahmey Abdalla Ali v. M.E.I. (F.C.T.D., no. A-572-92), Wetston, September 9, 1993.

Adjei v. Canada (Minister of Employment and Immigration), [1989] 2 F.C. 680 (C.A.)

Agimelen Oriazouwani, Winifred v. M.C.I. (F.C., no. IMM-6440-10), Shore, July 8, 2011; 2011 FC 827.

Aguilar Soto, Rafael Alberto v. M.C.I. (F.C., no. IMM-1883-10), Shore, November 25, 2010.

Ahmed v. Canada (Minister of Employment and Immigration) (1993), 156 N.R. 221 (F.C.A.)

Ahmed, Ahmed Ibrahim v. M.C.I. (F.C. no. IMM-2187-18), Kane, November 16, 2018; 2018 FC 1157.

Ahmed, Ali v. M.E.I. (F.C.A., no. A-89-92), Marceau, Desjardins, Décary, July 14, 1993.

Ahmed, Ishtiaq v. M.C.I. (F.C.T.D., no. IMM-2931-99), Hansen, March 29, 2000.

Ahoua, Wadjams Jean-Marie v. M.C.I. (F.C., no. IMM-1757-07), Blais, November 27, 2007; 2007 FC 1239.

Ajelal, Mustafa v. M.C.I. (F.C., no. IMM-4522-13), Diner, November 19, 2014; 2014 FC 1093.

Akpojiyovwi, Evelyn Oboaguonona v. M.C.I. (F.C. no. IMM-200-18), Roussel, July 17, 2018; 2018 FC 745.

Alassouli, Yousf v. M.C.I. (F.C., no. IMM-6451-10), de Montigny, August 16, 2011; 2011 FC 998.

Alfaro, Oscar Luis Alfaro v. M.C.I. (F.C., no. IMM-6905-03), O'Keefe, January 20, 2005.

Ali, Chaudhary Liaqat v. M.E.I. (F.C.T.D., no. A-1461-92), Noël, January 20, 1994.

Alvapillai, Ramasethu v. M.C.I. (F.C.T.D., no. IMM-4226-97), Rothstein, August 14, 1998.

Ambrose-Esede, Benedicta Osemen v. M.C.I. (F.C. no. IMM-1685-18), Russell, December 11, 2018; 2018 FC 1241.

Araya, Carolina Isabel Valenzuela v. M.C.I. (F.C.T.D., no. IMM-3948-97), Gibson, September 4, 1998

Aria, Ashraf v. M.C.I. (F.C., no. IMM-2499-12), de Montigny, April 2, 2013; 2013 FC 324.

Arias Aguilar, Jennifer v. M.C.I. (F.C., no. IMM-1000-05), Rouleau, November 9, 2005; 2005 FC 1519.).

Arias Ultima, Angela Maria v. M.C.I. (F.C., no. IMM-3984-12), Manson, January 25, 2013; 2013 FC 81.

Ascencio Gutierrez, Arnoldo Maximilanov. M.C.I. (F.C., no. IMM-4903-13)

Asfaw, Napoleon v. M.C.I. (F.C.T.D., no. IMM-5552-99), Hugessen, July 18, 2000

Ashraf, Shahenaz v. M.C.I. (F.C., no. IMM-5375-08), O'Reilly, April 19, 2010; 2010 FC 425

Aslam, Muhammad v. M.C.I. (F.C., no. IMM-3264-05), Shore, February 16, 2006; 2006 FC 189

Assadi, Nasser Eddin v. M.C.I. (F.C.T.D., no. IMM-2683-96), Teitelbaum, March 25, 1997.

Ay, Hasan v. M.C.I. (F.C., no. IMM-4149-09), Boivin, June 21, 2010; 2010 FC 671.

Badesha v. Canada (Secretary of State) (1994), 23 Imm. L.R. (2d) 190 (F.C.T.D.).

Badesha, Jagir Singh v. S.S.C. (F.C.T.D., no. A-1544-92), Wetston, January 19, 1994.

Badran, Housam v. M.C.I. (F.C.T.D., no. IMM-2472-95), McKeown, March 29, 1996

Bakos, Robert v. M.C.I. (F.C., no. IMM-2424-15), Manson, February 12, 2016 (amended September 7, 2016); 2016 FC 191

Balasubramaniam, Veergathy v. M.C.I. (F.C.T.D., no. IMM-1902-93), McKeown, October 4, 1994.

Barragan Gonzalez, Julio Angelo v. M.C.I. (F.C., no. IMM-6335-13), Boswell, April 20, 2015; 2015 FC 502.

Bello, Salihou v. M.C.I. (F.C.T.D., no. IMM-1771-96), Pinard, April 11, 1997.

Boakye, Kofi v. M.C.I. (F.C., no. IMM-2361-15), Strickland, December 18, 2015; 2015 FC 1394

Boston, Edwin v. M.C.I. (F.C., no. IMM-6554-06), Snider, December 4, 2007; 2007 FC 1271.

Caballero, Fausto Ramon Reyes v. M.E.I. (F.C.A., no. A-266-91), Marceau (dissenting), Desjardins, Létourneau, May 13, 1993.

Cadena Ramirez, Francisco José v. M.C.I. (F.C., no. IMM-5911-09), Rennie, December 20, 2010; 2010 FC 1276.

Canada (Attorney General) v. Ward, [1993] 2 S.C.R. 689, 103 D.L.R. (4th) 1, 20 Imm. L.R. (2d) 85

Canada (Minister of Citizenship and Immigration) v. Kadenko (1996), 143 D.L.R. (4th) 532 (F.C.A.)

Canada (Minister of Citizenship and Immigration) v. Patel, Dhruv Navichandra (F.C., no. IMM-2482-07), Lagacé, June 17, 2008; 2008 FC 747.

Canada (Minister of Employment and Immigration) v. Satiacum (1989), 99 N.R. 171 (F.C.A.).

Canada (Minister of Employment and Immigration) v. Sharbdeen (1994), 23 Imm. L.R. (2d) 300 (F.C.A.)

Cartagena, Wilber Orlando v. M.C.I. (F.C., no. IMM-961-06), Mosley, March 4, 2008; 2008 FC 289.

Chand, Mool v. M.C.I. (F.C., no. IMM-61-14), Rennie, February 19, 2015; 2015 FC 212.

Chandrakumar v. M.E.I. (F.C.T.D., no. A-1649-92), Pinard, May 16, 1997

Chauhdry, Mukhtar Ahmed v. M.C.I. (F.C.T.D., no. IMM-3951-97), Wetston, August 17, 1998.

Chaves, Alejandro Jose Martinez v. M.C.I. (F.C., no. IMM-603-04), Tremblay-Lamer, February 8, 2005; 2005 FC 193.

Chebli-Haj-Hassam v. Canada (Minister of Citizenship and Immigration) (1996), 36 Imm. L.R. (2d) 112 (F.C.A.).

Chebli-Haj-Hassam, Atef v. M.C.I. (F.C.A., no. A-191-95), Marceau, MacGuigan, Décary, May 28, 1996.

Chkiaou, Dimitri v. M.C.I. (F.C.T.D., no., IMM-266-94), Cullen, March 7, 1995.

Chudinov, Nickolai v. M.C.I. (F.C.T.D., no. IMM-2419-97), Joyal, August 14, 1998.

Dhaliwal, Jasbir Singh v. M.E.I. (F.C.T.D., no. 93-A-364), MacKay, August 9, 1993.

5, 1993.

Fernando, Joseph Stanley v. M.E.I. (F.C.T.D., no. 92-A-6986), McKeown, May 19, 1993.

Fosu, Frank Atta v. M.C.I. (F.C., no. IMM-935-08), Zinn, October 8, 2008; 2008 FC 1135.

Gabeyehu, Bruck v. M.C.I. (F.C.T.D., no. IMM-863-95), Reed, November 8, 1995.

Gallo Farias, Alejandrina Dayna v. M.C.I. (F.C., no. IMM-658-08), Kelen, September 16, 2008; 2008 FC 1035.

Garcia Aldana, Paco Jesus v. M.C.I. (F.C., no. IMM-2113-06), Hughes, April 19, 2007.

Gebremichael, Addis v. M.C.I. (F.C., no. IMM-2670-05), Russell, May 1, 2006; 2006 FC 547

Geron, Fernando Bilog v. M.C.I. (F.C.T.D., no. IMM-4951-01), Blanchard, November 22, 2002; 2002 FCT 1204.

Gomez Gonzalez, Veronica v. M.C.I. (F.C., no. IMM-485-11), de Montigny, October 4, 2011

Gomez v. Canada (Minister of Citizenship and Immigration) (F.C., IMM-1412-10), Bédard, October 22, 2010

Gonzalez Camargo, Hernando v. M.C.I. (F.C., no. IMM-38-14), Gleeson, September 2, 2015; 2015 FC 1044.

Gonzalez Torres, Luis Felipe v. M.C.I. (F.C., no. IMM-1351-09), Zinn, March 1, 2010; 2010 FC 234

Gopalapillai, Thinesrupan v. M.C.I. (F.C. no. IMM-3539-18), Grammond, February 26, 2019; 2019 FC 228

Gosal, Pardeep Singh v. M.C.I. (F.C.T.D., no. IMM-2316-97), Reed, March 11, 1998.

Guraya, Balihar Singh v. S.S.C. (F.C.T.D., no. IMM-4058-93), Pinard, July 8, 1994.

Gyawali, Nirmal v. M.C.I. (F.C., no. IMM-926-03), Tremblay-Lamer, September 24, 2003; 2003 FC 1122

Hasa, Ana v. M.C.I. (F.C., no. IMM-3700-17), Strickland, March 7, 2018; 2018 FC 270.

Hashmat, Suhil v. M.C.I. (F.C.T.D., no. IMM-2331-96), Teitelbaum, May 9, 1997.

Hasnain, Khalid v. M.C.I. (F.C.T.D., no. A-962-92), McKeown, December 14, 1995.

Hassan, Liban v. M.E.I. (F.C.T.D., no. IMM-3634-98), Campbell, April 14, 1999.

Hatami, Arezo v. M.C.I. (F.C.T.D., no. IMM-2418-98), Lemieux, March 23, 2000

Helen v. M.C.I. (F.C., no. IMM-6120-11), Rennie, April 10, 2012; 2012 FC 399.

Hernandez Cardozo, Eduardo v. M.C.I. (F.C., no. IMM-5095-11), Shore, February 9, 2012; 2012 FC 190.

Herrera, Juan Blas Perez de Corcho v. M.E.I. (F.C.T.D., no. A-615-92), Noël, October 19, 1993

Herrera, William Alexander Cruz v. M.C.I. (F.C., IMM-782-07), Beaudry, October 1, 2007

Hidalgo Tranquino, Claudia Isabel v. M.C.I. (F.C., no. IMM-86-10), Mactavish, July 29, 2010; 2010 FC 793

Hinzman, Jeremy v. M.C.I. and (F.C.A, no. A-182-06)

Huerta v. Canada (Minister of Employment and Immigration) (1993), 157 N.R. 225 (F.C.A.).

Hughey, Brandon David v. M.C.I. (F.C.A. no. A-185-06)

I.M.P.P. v. M.C.I. (F.C., no. IMM-4049-09), Mosley, March 9, 2010; 2010 FC 259.

Ibrahimov, Fikrat v. M.C.I. (F.C., no. IMM-4258-02), Heneghan, October 10, 2003; 2003 FC 1185.

Idahosa, Musili Amoke v. M.C.I. (F.C. no. IMM-1124-18), Favel, March 29, 2019; 2019 FC 384.

Idrees, Muhammad v. M.C.I. (F.C., no. IMM-4136-13), Diner, December 10, 2014; 2014 FC 1194.

Idris, Omer Mahmoud Hussein v. M.C.I. (F.C. no. IMM-2321-18), Brown, January 9, 2019; 2019 FC 24.

Ioda v. Canada (Minister of Employment and Immigration) (1993), 21 Imm. L.R. (2d) 294 (F.C.T.D.)

Ioda, Routa v. M.E.I. (F.C.T.D., no. 92-A-6604)

Ismayilov, Anar v. M.C.I. (F.C., no. IMM-7263-14), Mactavish, August 26, 2015; 2015 FC 1013.

Isufi, Arlind v. M.C.I. (F.C., no. IMM-5631-02), Tremblay-Lamer, July 15, 2003

Jeyachandran, Senthan v. S.G.C. (F.C.T.D., no. IMM-799-94), McKeown, March 30, 1995.

Jilani, Zia Uddin Ahmed v. M.C.I. (F.C., no. IMM-711-07), Mosley, December 21, 2007; 2007 FC 1354

John, Shontel Dion v. M.C.I. (F.C., no. IMM-1683-10), Bédard, December 14, 2010; 2010 FC 1283

Kabengele v. M.C.I. (F.C. no., IMM-1422-99), Rouleau, November 16, 2000

Kahlon v. Canada (Solicitor General), (1993), 24 Imm. L.R. (2d) 219 (F.C.T.D.)

Kahlon, Hari Singh v. S.G.C (F.C.T.D., no. IMM-532-93), Gibson, August 5, 1993.

Kaillyapillai, Srivasan v. M.C.I. (F.C.T.D., no. IMM-1263-96), Richard, February 27, 1997.

Kaler, Minder Singh v. M.E.I. (F.C.T.D., no. IMM-794-93), Cullen, February 3, 1994.

Kamana, Jimmy v. M.C.I. (F.C.T.D., no. IMM-5998-98), Tremblay-Lamer, September 24, 1999.

Kanji, Mumtaz Baduraliv.M.C.I. (F.C.T.D., no. IMM-2451-96), Campbell, April 4, 1997.

Karthikesu, Cumariah v. M.E.I. (F.C.T.D., no. IMM-2998-93), Strayer, May 26, 1994.

Kauhonina, Claretha v. M.C.I. (F.C. no. IMM-2459-18), Diner, December 21, 2018; 2018 FC 1300.

Kayumba, Bijou Kamwanga v. M.C.I. (F.C., no. IMM-1920-09), Beaudry, February 10, 2010; 2010 FC 138.

Khan, Naqui Mohd v. M.C.I. (F.C.T.D., no. IMM-4127-01), Rothstein, July 26, 2002.

Khattr, Amani Khzaee v. M.C.I. (F.C. no., IMM-3249-15), Zinn, March 22, 2016; 2016 FC 341.

Kulanthavelu, Gnanasegaram v. M.E.I. (F.C.T.D., no. IMM-57-93), Gibson, December 3, 1993.

Kunin, Aleksandr v. M.C.I. (F.C., no. IMM-5225-09), O'Keefe, November 4, 2010; 2010 FC 1091

Kurtkapan, Osman v. M.C.I. (F.C.T.D., no. IMM-5290-01), Heneghan, October 25, 2002; 2002 FCT 1114

Li, Yi Mei v. M.C.I. (F.C.A., no. A-31-04), Rothstein, Noël, Malone, January 5, 2005; 2005 FCA 1.

August 14, 1998.

Megag, Sahra Abdilahi v. M.E.I. (F.C.T.D., no. A-822-92), Rothstein, December 10, 1993.

Mekideche, Anouar v. M.C.I. (F.C.T.D., no. IMM-2269-96), Wetston, December 9, 1996

Memarpour, Mahdi v. M.C.I. (F.C.T.D., no. IMM-3113-94), Simpson, May 25, 1995

Mendez, Alberto Luis Calderon v. (F.C., no. IMM-1837-04), Teitelbaum, January 27, 2005; 2005 FC 75.

Milian Pelaez, Rogelio v. M.C.I. (F.C., no. IMM-3611-11), de Montigny, March 2, 2012; 2012 FC 285

Mimica, Milanka v. M.C.I. (F.C.T.D., no. IMM-3014-95), Rothstein, June 19, 1996.

Moran Gudiel, Hugo v. M.C.I. (F.C., no. IMM-2054-14), Gascon, July 23, 2015; 2015 FC 902.

Moreb, Sliman v. M.C.I. (F.C., no. IMM-287-05), von Finckenstein, July 5, 2005; 2005 FC 945.

Moreno Maniero, Ronald Antonio v. M.C.I. (F.C., no. IMM-8536-11), Zinn, June 19, 2012; 2012 FC 776.

Mortocian, Alexandru v. M.C.I. (.FC. no., IMM-3837-12), Kane, December 7, 2012; 2012 FC 1447.

Moya, Jaime Olvera v. M.C.I. (F.C.T.D., no. IMM-5436-01), Beaudry, November 6, 2002.

Mudrak, Zsolt Jozsef v. M.C.I. (F.C.A., no. A-147-15), Stratas, Webb, Scott, June 14, 2016; 2016 FCA 178.

Muhammed, Falululla Peer v. M.C.I. (F.C., no. IMM-5122-11), Harrington, February 17, 2012; 2012 FC 226.

Muotoh, Ndukwe Christopher v. M.C.I. (F.C., no. IMM-3330-05)

Murillo Taborda, Lissed v. M.C.I. (F.C., no. IMM-9365-12), Kane, September 17, 2013; 2013 FC 957.

Nadarajah, Sivasothy Nathan v. M.E.I. (F.C.T.D., no. IMM-4215-93), Simpson, July 26, 1994.

Naguleswaran, Pathmasilosini (Naguleswaran) v. M.C.I. (F.C.T.D., no. IMM-1116-94), Muldoon, April 19, 1995.

Natynczyk v. Canada (Minister of Employment and Immigration), (F.C., no. IMM-2025-03)

Saini, Makhan Singh v. M.E.I. (F.C.A., no. A-750-91), Mahoney, Stone, Linden, March 22, 1993.

Salamanca, Miguel Angel Sandoval v. M.C.I. (F.C., no. IMM-6737-11), Zinn, June 19, 2012; 2012 FC 780.

Salguero, Erbin Salomon Rosales v. M.C.I. (F.C., no. IMM-4402-04), Mactavish, May 18, 2005; 2005 FC 716

Salibian v. Canada (Minister of Employment and Immigration), [1990] 3 F.C. 250 (C.A.).

Salvagno, Sergio Santiago Raymond v. M.C.I. (F.C., no. IMM-5848-10), *Pinard,* May 26, 2011; 2011 FC 595

Sanchez, Leonardo Gonzalez v. M.C.I. (F.C., no. IMM-3154-03), Mactavish, May 18, 2004; 2004 FC 731.

Sangha, Karamjit Singh v. M.C.I. (F.C.T.D., no. IMM-1555-98), Reed, October 28, 1998.

Sanno, Aminata v. M.C.I. (F.C.T.D., no. IMM-2124-95), Tremblay-Lamer, April 25, 1996.

Scott, Dailon Ronald v. M.C.I. (F.C., no. IMM-2691-12), Gagné, September 10, 2012; 2012 FC 1066.

Selvakumaran, Sivachelam v. M.C.I (F.C.T.D., no. IMM-5103-01), Mckeown, May 31, 2002

Shah, Mahmood Ali v. M.C.I. (F.C., no. IMM-4425-02), Blanchard, September 30, 2003; 2003 FC 1121

Shahpari, Khadijeh v. M.C.I. (F.C.T.D., no. IMM-2327-97), Rothstein, April 3, 1998.

Shaka, Abdul Shema v. M.C.I. (F.C., no. IMM-4141-11), Rennie, February 21, 2012; 2012 FC 235.

Shanmugarajah, Appiah v. M.E.I. (F.C.A., no. A-609-91), Stone, MacGuigan, Henry, June 22, 1992.

Siddiq, Dawood v. M.C.I. (F.C., no. IMM-1684-03), Harrington, March 31, 2004; 2004 FC 490.

Sidhu, Jadgish Singh v. M.E.I. (F.C.T.D., no. 92-A-6540), Muldoon, May 31, 1993.

Sikiratu Iyile, Sandra v. M.C.I. (F.C., no. IMM-6609-10), Harrington, July 25, 2011; 2011 FC 928.

Singh, (Gurmeet) v. Canada (Minister of Citizenship and Immigration) (1995), 30 Imm. L.R. (2d) 226 (F.C.T.D.)

Singh, Gurmeet v. M.C.I. (F.C.T.D., no. IMM-75-95), Richard, July 4, 1995.

Singh, Harminder v. M.C.I. (F.C`. no. IMM-4333-13), Gleason, March 20, 2014; 2014 FC 269.

Singh, Nirmal v. M.C.I. (F.C., no. IMM-7334-05), Teitelbaum, June 13, 2006, 2006 FC 743.

Singh, Ranjit v. M.C.I. (F.C.T.D., no. A-605-92), Reed, July 23, 1996.

Singh, Sebastian Swatandra v. M.C.I. (F.C.T.D., no. IMM-3840-97), Nadon, December 7, 1998

Singh, Sucha v. M.E.I. (F.C.T.D., no. 93-A-91), Dubé, June 23, 1993.

Singh, Swarn v. M.E.I. (F.C.T.D., no. A-1409-92), Rothstein, May 4, 1994.

Sivaraththinam, Mayooran v. M.C.I. (F.C., no. IMM-13174-12), Annis, February 20, 2014; 2014 FC 162

Sow, Harouna Sibo v. M.C.I., no. IMM-5287-10, Rennie, June 6, 2011; 2011 FC 646.

Syvyryn, Ganna v. M.C.I. (F.C., no. IMM-1569-09), Snider, October 13, 2009.

Tabet-Zatla, Mohamed v. *M.C.I.* (F.C.T.D., no. IMM-6291-98), Tremblay-Lamer, November 2, 1999.

Tahlil, Mohamed Sugule v. M.C.I. (F.C., no. IMM-5920-10), Zinn, July 5, 2011; 2011 FC 817.

Tang, Xiaoming v. M.C.I. (F.C.T.D., no. IMM-3650-99)

Tawfik v. Canada (Minister of Employment and Immigration) (1993), 26 Imm. L.R. (2d) 148 (F.C.T.D.).

Tawfik, Taha Mohammed v. M.E.I. (F.C.T.D., no. 93-A-311), MacKay, August 23, 1993.

Thabet v. Canada (Minister of Citizenship and Immigration), [1998] 4 F.C. 21 (C.A.).

Thevarajah, Anton Felix v. M.C.I. (F.C., no. IMM-695-04), Mosley, November 24, 2004; 2004 FC 1654.

Thevasagayam, Ebenezer Thevaraj v. M.C.I. (F.C.T.D., no. IMM-252-97), Tremblay-Lamer, October 23, 1997.

Thirunavukkarasu v. Canada (Minister of Employment and Immigration), [1994] 1 F.C. 589 (C.A.).

Troya Jimenez, Jose Walter v. M.C.I. (F.C., no. IMM-128-10)

Uppal, Jatinder Singh v. M.C.I. (F.C.A., no. A-42-94), Isaac, Hugessen,

Décary, November 1, 1994.

Uppal, Jatinder Singh v. S.S.C. (F.C.T.D., no. A-17-93), Wetston, January 19, 1994.

Vaitialingam v. M.C.I. (F.C., no. IMM-9445-03), O'Keefe, October 20, 2004, 2004 FCT 1459

Velasco Moreno, Sebastian v. M.C.I. (F.C., no. IMM-454-10), Lutfy, October 5, 2010; 2010 FC 993.

Velez, Liliana v. M.C.I. (F.C., no. IMM-5660-09), Crampton, September 15, 2010; 2010 FC 923

Vidal, Daniel Fernando v. M.E.I. (F.C.T.D., no. A-644-92), Gibson, May 15, 1997.

Voyvodov, Bogdan Atanassov v. M.C.I. (F.C.T.D., no. IMM-5601-98), Lutfy, September 13, 1999

Yoganathan, Kandasamy v. M.C.I. (F.C.T.D., no. IMM-3588-97), Gibson, April 20, 1998.

Yuan, Xin v. M.C.I. (F.C., no. IMM-5365-14), Boswell, July 28, 2015; 2015 FC 923

Yusuf v. Canada (Minister of Employment and Immigration), [1992] 1 F.C. 629 (C.A.), at 632.

Zalzali v. Canada (Minister of Employment and Immigration), [1991] 3 F.C. 605 (C.A.).

Zamora Huerta, Erika Angelina v. M.C.I. (F.C., no. IMM-1985-07), Blanchard, May 8, 2008; 2008 FC 586.

Zaytoun, Hussein v. M.C.I. (F.C., no. IMM-1769-14), Mactavish, October 2, 2014; 2014 FC 939.

Zetino v. Canada (Minister of Citizenship and Immigration) (1994), 25 Imm. L.R. (2d) 300 (F.C.T.D.)

Zetino, Rudys Francisco Mendoza v. M.C.I. (F.C.T.D., no. IMM-6173-93), Cullen, October 13, 1994.

Zewedu, Haimanot v. M.C.I. (F.C.T.D., no. IMM-5564-99), Hugessen, July 18, 2000

Zuniga, Alexis Ramon Garciav. S.C.C. (F.C.T.D., no. IMM-118-94), Teitelbaum, July 4, 1994.

INTRODUCTION

Questions that come before the Refugee Protection Division (RPD) of the Immigration and Refugee Board (IRB) are known as *issues*. There are, generally, any number of issues that may come before an adjudicator, also known as a Tribunal or Board or Panel or Member, and these may include founded fear of persecution, state protection, IFA, re-availment, delay in making a claim, credibility (of documents, story, etc.), etc. Credibility is always an issue in Nigerian refugee claims.

This book is for those who would like to make a successful refugee claim in Canada from Nigeria. Canada gathers relevant information from specific countries and organizes it in a series of documents known as National Documentation Package (NDP). For Nigeria, its NDP[1] was current as of May 31st, 2023. This information is periodically updated. Thus, Nigerian claimants are advised to consult this material and refer to the latest information before or during the claim process.

---

[1]https://irb.gc.ca/en/country-information/ndp/Pages/index.aspx?pid=11820 accessed on October 9th, 2023.

In addition, this book is an introduction to the refugee determination system (RDS) in Canada. Refugee claims may be based on political, religious, sexual orientation, or gender-related persecutions. The principles applicable to religious or political or gender-related persecutions can be applied to the other grounds.[2]

Nigerians face credibility issues in their refugee claim bids. Credibility is the issue regardless of whether the claim arises in any of the following areas: Female Genital Mutilations (FGM); sexual-orientation; or traditional (or cultural) chieftaincy inheritance. The four most common issues of a refugee claim for protection in Canada are credibility, founded fear of persecution, internal flight alternatives (IFA), and state protection. Credibility is always presumed until rebutted.

Other issues include delay, re-availment and refugee surplace. Many Nigerian refugee claimants are able to excel on the above, except for credibility reasons. And credibility, in so far as Nigeria is concerned, is focused on two areas: Credibility of documents and credibility of the story.

---

[2] See Chapter 1 on page 2

Credibility of documents is a very important area of refugee findings.[3] The experience and history of Nigerian claimants has not helped. Nigeria is, perhaps, the worst country on the Canadian radar when it comes to credibility. In the past, Nigerians have been alleged to have fabricated documents and even doctored them, collaborating with corrupt officials and interests in Nigeria to corruptly "create" documents.

Documents here include national identity documents; voters' cards; accreditation documents for lawyers and notaries; police certificates and abstracts; educational credentials; medical letters, certificates and prognoses; and even immigration documents (passports; Visas, etc.).

Credibility of story makes or breaks a Nigerian refugee claim. The nature of the Nigerian society and the history of corruption make it difficult for adjudicators to limit themselves to simple questions limited to the Basis of Claim (BOC) narrative. Adjudicators find themselves probing on all fronts, including the areas not specifically mentioned in the BOC narrative. This makes it extremely difficult for Nigerian claimants to prepare adequately for the knowledge test. Some adjudicators may completely ignore the BOC narrative (story) and probe on areas claimants did not expect. This has caused Nigerian claim failure rates to spike.[4]

---

[3] See Chapter 8
[4] See the dialogue box in Chapter 5

This book provides the necessary strategies to increase the chances of succeeding in a refugee claim for Nigerian claimants in two ways. First, Nigerian refugee claimants and their counsels will be ready to request and review authentic documents originating from Nigeria. This will reduce unnecessary clogging on document assessment and review.

And second, claimants and counsels will know how to prepare for the knowledge test – by not only limiting themselves to the BOC story, but by understanding the entire scope of the requirements for knowledge test on a Nigerian-originated refugee claim.

1 | REFUGEE DETERMINATION

> The Canadian refugee determination system relies heavily on international law – conventions and protocols. The federal law under which it falls has domesticated most, if not, all international treaties pertaining to matters of refugees.

C anada protects and grants refugee statuses to people who are fleeing persecution from their countries of origin (of citizenship) or of their former habitual residence. Canada is a signatory to the United Nations conventions[5] that variously protect people who are not able to be protected in their own countries of citizenships or of former habitual residence due to political, religious, gender or other factors.

---

[5] Such as the "The Convention Relating to the Status of Refugees" also known as the 1951 Refugee Convention; and the Protocol Relating to the Status of Refugees (also known as 1967 Protocol). The 1967 Protocol came into force on October 4th, 1967. It had 146 parties. Canada became a signatory on June 4th, 1969.

United Nations Refugee Convention

Article 1 of the 1951 the United Nations Refugee Convention (the "Refugee Convention") defines a refugee as one:

> ...owing to **well-founded fear** of being persecuted for reasons of **race, religion, nationality, membership of a particular social group or political opinion**, is **outside the country** of his nationality and is unable or, owing to such fear, is **unwilling to avail himself of the protection of that country**; or who, not having a nationality and being outside the country of his former **habitual residence** as a result of such events, is unable or, owing to such fear, is **unwilling to return to it.**[6]

---

[6] *Ibid.* (Emphasis added)

Founded Fear of Persecution

As emphasized above, not all people fleeing their home countries qualify to be refugees. A refugee must have a well-founded fear of persecution in their home country (country of citizenship or of former habitual residence). This fear must be genuine.

However, it must not be a proven fear. It is enough that a person believes that they are in danger of persecution. The fear is such that the Claimant risks being persecuted if returned to their country of citizenship.

Incidental Factors to Convention Refugee Claims

Fear alone is not enough; it must be based on five key grounds:[7] Race, religion, nationality (national origin or ancestry), membership in a particular social group; and political opinion. Outside of these itemized grounds (or grounds associated to these), a nation may not have the necessary jurisdiction to grant protection to a refugee claimant.

---

[7] It is trite law in Canada to be found a refugee or protected person on only one ground even if more than one grounds equally apply.

Moreover, one has to be "outside" of their country of citizenship or of former habitual residence in order to claim for refugee protection. The country of citizenship or former habitual residence must be unwilling or unable to avail the refugee claimant protection.

Domestication of UN Conventions

Canada has domesticated most United Nations (UN) conventions, including the one that protects refugees. To **domesticate** a convention is to translate it into national law so that in letter as in spirit, the convention is applicable to the local or national environment. *The Immigration Refugee Protection Act* ("IRPA"),[8] the Immigration and Refugee Protection Regulations,[9] the *Constitution*[10] and the *Citizenship Act*[11] and its regulations, govern immigration, refugees and citizenship matters in Canada. In Canada, immigration and refugee matters fall under federal jurisdiction.[12]

---

[8] (S.C. 2001, c. 27)
[9] (SOR/2002-227)
[10] The *Constitution Act*, 1982
[11] S.C. 1946, c. 15
[12] Section 91 of the Constitution

Once a nation domesticates or contracts or otherwise becomes a signatory to the UN Refugee Convention, it takes on the responsibility of protecting and fulfilling certain obligations for the claimant. Mandatory obligations of the contracting nations include exempting refugee claimants from reciprocity;[13] providing security; transferring marriages and providing free access to courts.

Other general obligations include administrative (paperwork) assistance; travel document assistance and transfer of assets assistance; assimilating and naturalizing refugees; and so on. In fulfilling these obligations, contracting nations must not discriminate, or forcibly return or "refoul" refugees to the country of their danger,[14] and so on.

---

[13] Article 7 (2) of Refugee Convention 1951, "After a period of three years' residence, all refugees shall enjoy exemption from legislative reciprocity in the territory of the Contracting States." Legislative Reciprocity has been defined as: "The phrasing of Article 7 (2) constitutes an attempt to restore a balance between those rights and benefits which a State may be prepared to grant to any alien (and where consequently the rule of reciprocity only is a means of achieving equal rights and benefits for one's own nationals abroad); those rights and benefits which are meant to be an exclusive privilege for certain foreign nationals" (Commentary on the Refugee Convention 1951 ARTICLES 2-11, 13-37, published by the Division of International Protection of the United Nations High Commissioner for Refugees, 1997)

[14] See Article 33 of the UN Refugee Convention

On June 4th, 1969, Canada signed the UN Refugee Convention, "18 years after it was adopted by the United Nations. Since Canada signed the Refugee Convention, it has gained the enviable reputation of being a world leader in protecting refugees."[15]

Because Canada has appended its signature to the UN Refugee Convention that requires that such people be granted a safe haven in Canada, Canada cannot, therefore, return them to the countries to which they claim that they are or will be in danger of being persecuted.

Non-Refoulement

The doctrine that prevents countries like Canada from returning refugees to countries they claim they would face persecution is called **Non-Refoulement**. **Persecution** is generally defined in this book as torture or threat of torture, unlawful criminal charges or arrest (with or without a warrant), detentions (with or without trials), and death.

---

[15] Canadian Council for Refugees, "Recognizing successes, acting for change," < https://ccrweb.ca/sites/ccrweb.ca/files/static-files/40thanniversary.htm> (Accessed on November 22nd, 2019)

Canadian Refugee Determination System

The immigration and refugee system in Canada comprises (1) The Immigration, Refugees and Citizenship Canada (**IRCC**, formerly Citizenship and Immigration Canada or **CIC**); (2) The Canada Border Services Agency or **CBSA**. (The CBSA is part of the Government of Canada's public safety portfolio. It is an agency of Public Safety and Emergency Preparedness Canada (PSEPC)); and (3) the Immigration and Refugee Board of Canada (**IRB**).

This book does not discuss the IRCC and the CBSA, except mentioning in passing that the IRCC deals with all immigration matters, including granting Visas and permits, sponsorship applications and other aspects of immigration such as temporary residence, permanent residence, business immigration, express entry or humanitarian and compassionate (H&C) considerations. The responsibility of CBSA includes requesting detention reviews, and effecting deportations from Canada, but not adjudicating detention reviews.

The IRB is divided into 4 divisions: The Immigration Division (ID); the Immigration Appeal Division (IAD); the Refugee Protection Division (RPD); and the Refugee Appeal Division (RAD). Special adjudicators called **Members** make decisions at the IRB. A claimant at the IRB may be represented by counsel. **Counsel** means a lawyer. The IRB has extended the meaning of counsel to representatives who are recognized under s.91/2 of the IRPA, and these include Licensed Paralegals and Immigration Consultants.

The meaning of counsel, therefore, denotes representatives who have been licensed either by the Law Society of their respective provincial law regulatory bodies or by the federal immigration consultant's regulatory body. All paid representatives must be verified by the IRB. Previously, they submitted a form called **Counsel Contact Information** in which they provided their membership number. Presently, they must be registered in a portal called My Case.[16] Counsel must also submit an immigration form called **Use of a Representative**.

The two forms and the portal require counsel to provide their membership number, contact details (addresses of their offices, telephone numbers, fax numbers or even email addresses).

---

[16] https://my-case-mon-dossier.irb-cisr.gc.ca/en-US/ accessed on October 10th, 2023

The Use of a Representative form also requires the claimant to cancel the representative should that need arise. Once the IRB has received the Counsel Contact Information form or the Use of a Representative form, or the portal has been created, the RPD will then correspond with counsel as well as the claimant.

This author has represented all kinds of Nigerian refugee claimants in Canada. He has both observed and experienced the key credibility issues that arise in such claims. And since refugee law is quintessentially administrative law, the complete and consistent following of procedure is part of the success both counsel and the claimant want at the IRB.

2 | UNITED NATIONS CONVENTIONS

> Both the United Nations (UN) conventions and protocols, and the Canadian immigration and refugee laws only protect people who are fleeing from *persecution*, and *not* necessarily from discrimination.

Persecution v. Discrimination

The United Nations Convention Relating to the Status of Refugees (hereinafter, the "Refugee Convention"),[17] is described as a human rights instrument.[18] However, it remains a human rights instrument as it requires contracting states not to discriminate in terms of who they accept or reject as a refugee. The grounds for seeking asylum (or making a refugee claim) themselves are not subject to human rights prognosis.

---

[17] Adopted on July 28th, 1951.
[18] <https://www.ohchr.org/en/instruments-mechanisms/instruments/convention-relating-status-refugees> accessed on October 9th, 2023.

In its non-discrimination clause,[19] the Refugee Convention states that: "The Contracting States shall apply the provisions of this Convention to refugees without discrimination as to race, religion, or country of origin."[20]

The 1967 Protocol on Refugees (the "Refugee Protocol")[21] is a supplement to the Refugee Convention. The Refugee Protocol states, thus, "'refugee' shall…mean any person within the definition of article I of the [Refugee] Convention."

Article I of the Refugee Convention is an omnibus provision that defines a refugee and provides areas or reasons that might bar one from being a refugee, as follows:

> A. For the purposes of the present Convention, the term "refugee" shall apply to any person who:
>
> (1) Has been considered a refugee under the Arrangements of 12 May 1926 and 30 June 1928 or under the Conventions of 28 October 1933 and 10 February 1938, the Protocol of 14 September 1939 or the Constitution of the International Refugee Organization;

---

[19] Article 3 of Refugee Convention
[20] Ibid.
[21] < https://www.ohchr.org/en/instruments-mechanisms/instruments/protocol-relating-status-refugees> accessed on October 9th, 2023.

Decisions of non-eligibility taken by the International Refugee Organization during the period of its activities shall not prevent the status of refugee being accorded to persons who fulfil the conditions of paragraph 2 of this section;

(2) As a result of events occurring before 1 January 1951 and *owing to well-founded fear of being persecuted for reasons of* **race, religion, nationality, membership of a particular social group** *or* **political opinion**, *is outside the country of his nationality and is unable or, owing to such fear, is unwilling to avail himself of the protection of that country; or who, not having a nationality and being outside the country of his former habitual residence as a result of such events, is unable or, owing to such fear, is unwilling to return to it.*

In the case of a person who has more than one nationality, the term "the country of his nationality" shall mean each of the countries of which he is a national, and a person shall not be deemed to be lacking the protection of the country of his nationality if, without any valid reason based on well-founded fear, he has not availed himself of the protection of one of the countries of which he is a national.

B. (1) For the purposes of this Convention, the words "events occurring before 1 January 1951" in article 1, section A, shall be understood to mean either (a) "events occurring in Europe before 1 January 1951"; or (b) "events occurring in Europe or elsewhere before 1 January 1951"; and each Contracting State shall make a declaration at the time of signature, ratification or accession, specifying which of these meanings it applies for the purpose of its obligations under this Convention.
(2) Any Contracting State which has adopted alternative (a) may at any time extend its obligations by adopting alternative (b) by means of a notification addressed to the Secretary-General of the United Nations.

C. This Convention shall cease to apply to any person falling under the terms of section A if:
(1) He has voluntarily re-availed himself of the protection of the country of his nationality; or
(2) Having lost his nationality, he has voluntarily reacquired it; or
(3) He has acquired a new nationality, and enjoys the protection of the country of his new nationality; or
(4) He has voluntarily re-established himself in the country which he left or outside which he remained owing to fear of persecution; or

(5) He can no longer, because the circumstances in connection with which he has been recognized as a refugee have ceased to exist, continue to refuse to avail himself of the protection of the country of his nationality; provided that this paragraph shall not apply to a refugee falling under section A (1) of this article who is able to invoke compelling reasons arising out of previous persecution for refusing to avail himself of the protection of the country of nationality;

(6) Being a person who has no nationality he is, because the circumstances in connection with which he has been recognized as a refugee have ceased to exist, able to return to the country of his former habitual residence; provided that this paragraph shall not apply to a refugee falling under section A (1) of this article who is able to invoke compelling reasons arising out of previous persecution for refusing to return to the country of his former habitual residence.

D. This Convention shall not apply to persons who are at present receiving from organs or agencies of the United Nations other than the United Nations High Commissioner for Refugees protection or assistance. When such protection or assistance has ceased for any reason, without the position of such persons being definitively settled in accordance with the relevant resolutions adopted by the General Assembly of the United Nations, these persons shall ipso facto be entitled to the benefits of this Convention.

E. This Convention shall not apply to a person who is recognized by the competent authorities of the country in which he has taken residence as having the rights and obligations which are attached to the possession of the nationality of that country.

F. The provisions of this Convention shall not apply to any person with respect to whom there are serious reasons for considering that:
(a) He has committed a crime against peace, a war crime, or a crime against humanity, as defined in the international instruments drawn up to make provision in respect of such crimes;
(b) He has committed a serious non-political crime outside the country of refuge prior to his admission to that country as a refugee;

(c) He has been guilty of acts contrary to the purposes and principles of the United Nations.[22]

The "definition of a convention refugee states that a claimant's fear of persecution must be 'by reason of' one of the five enumerated grounds - that is race, religion, nationality, membership in a particular social group and political opinion."[23]

The Refugee Convention as does the Refugee Protocol by extension, recognizes five (5) grounds of persecution: Race, religion, nationality, membership of a particular social group or political opinion.

"Membership of a particular social group" is broadly defined and, for Nigeria, may include areas such as sexual orientation, rape and women abuse, traditional issues of chieftaincy, Female Genital Mutilations (FGM), and areas incidental to these.

Refugee claims are not based on sympathy or humanitarian factors. They are strictly legal. It is common for claimants to argue their despondency, destitution, or desperation at the RPD. That is not the jurisdiction of refugee institutions. They are not set up to sympathize with people, generally. A claimant must establish that they meet the requirements of the law.

---

[22] Emphasis added.

[23] See IRB - Chapter 4 - Grounds of persecution – Nexus; *Canada (Attorney General) v. Ward*, [1993] 2 S.C.R. 689, 103 D.L.R. (4th) 1, 20 Imm. L.R. (2d) 85 at 732; *Chan v. Canada (Minister of Employment and Immigration)*, [1993] 3 F.C. 675; (1993), 20 Imm. L.R. (2d) 181 (C.A.), at 689-690 and 692-693.

There must be a link or *nexus* between the fear of *persecution* and one of the above five grounds. This nexus, however, does not seem to extend to poverty or other forms of discrimination. Claimants must be careful to delineate discrimination from persecution otherwise their claim may fail. Thus, fleeing one's country to seek a good life for them or their family does not form any nexus to any of the five grounds of refugee claim in Canada. Such claims are doomed to fail on arrival.

The language in the Refugee Convention, thus, "refugees without discrimination as to race, religion, or country of origin," is sometimes misconstrued to mean discrimination *per se*. Both the Refugee Convention and the Refugee Protocol which Canada adopted,[24] do not involve discrimination, although in spirit, they are clearly human rights instruments. When applied to individual nations such as to Canada, a refugee claim must be based on "persecution" and not "discrimination." Canada does not have jurisdiction to protect individuals fleeing from their countries of origin due to discrimination.

Even the quintessential human rights treaty, the Universal Declaration of Human Rights, makes this clear distinction:

> (1) Everyone has the right to seek and to enjoy in other countries asylum from *persecution*.

---

[24] See section 96 and subsection 97(1) of the *Immigration and Refugee Protection Act, supra.*

(2) This *right* may not be invoked in the case of prosecutions genuinely arising from non-political crimes or from acts contrary to the purposes and principles of the United Nations.[25]

Who is Not a Refugee

In tandem with the Refugee Convention, Article 14 of the Universal Declaration of Human Rights illustrates two important facets of refugee protection. First, that the refugee conventions only apply with respect to refugees fleeing *persecution* from their countries of origin or of habitual residence, and not fleeing discrimination.

Persecution is defined as hostility and ill-treatment, especially on the basis of ethnicity, religion, or sexual orientation or political beliefs.[26] Persecution is more than discrimination; it is a very severe form of discrimination. It results in the denial or infringement of *fundamental rights*.

Discrimination, on the other hand, is the treatment that favors one at the expense of another based on a protected characteristic, in an area recognized as a public domain. Persecution is, by degree and form, a worse form of discrimination.

---

[25] Article 14 of UN Universal Declaration of Human Rights (1948), emphasis added.
[26] Oxford Languages Dictionary

There is a frequent juxtaposition of discrimination and persecution in HIV/AIDS-related claims from Nigerian claimants. Unless otherwise indicated with clear evidence, HIV-AIDS marginalization may or may not rise to the level of persecution. Indeed, HIV-AIDS patients are frequently discriminated against, especially in access to healthcare in Nigeria.

The stigma associated with the illness may force some traditionally-oriented citizenry to pour scorn on HIV-AIDS sufferers. And this may rise to the level of persecution in some resects. Any claimant advancing this theory must be cogent, deliberate, and clear in the presentation of their evidence before the Refugee Protection Division (RPD) of the Canadian Immigration and Refugee Board (IRB).

Second and last, claimants fleeing persecution must establish that they were or are not able to be availed **state protection** by the Nigerian government. Government in Nigeria may include federal, state, traditional or municipality. Like with discrimination, Canada does not protect people who are fleeing persecution due to the actions of non-state actors unless that non-state actor is a recognized gang, traditional authority or a group identified within organized criminality.

The five[27] identified grounds of persecution which may give rise to a refugee claim are deemed to exclude persecutions because of serious criminality. Political crimes are excepted. Non-political crimes are not excepted.

Article I(F)(a)-(c) states: "The provisions of this Convention shall not apply to any person with respect to whom there are *serious reasons* for considering that: (a) He has *committed* a crime against *peace, a war crime, or a crime against humanity*, as defined in the international instruments drawn up to make provision in respect of such crimes; (b) He has *committed a serious non-political crime outside the country of refuge prior to his admission to that country as a refugee*; (c) He has been *guilty* of acts contrary to the purposes and principles of the United Nations."

The provisions above, exclude convicts of serious non-political crimes in or outside Canada from seeking asylum or making a refugee claim in Canada. In making arguments regarding these provisions, the focus is usually on "serious" crimes. In a recent case[28] by this author at the Refugee Appeal Division (RAD) of IRB, the claimant successfully won on appeal. The adjudicator agreed with the position of this author that the appellant's criminal convictions in the US did not arise to the level of serious criminality in Canada. The case was referred back for redetermination by a different panel.

---

[27] Race, religion, nationality, membership in a particular social group and political opinion
[28] TC2-37888 (2023)

The Refugee Convention eliminates another unit of claimants from making refugee claims in Canada. These include **re-availed** claimants. These are those who initially enter Canada voluntarily and voluntarily return to the countries where they claim to be persecuted: "He has voluntarily re-availed himself of the protection of the country of his nationality."[29]

The other is those who initially lost the citizenship of their original countries and have now reacquired it: "Having lost his nationality, he has voluntarily reacquired it."[30]

The list also includes he who has "acquired a new nationality and enjoys the protection of the country of his new nationality."[31]

Those who have "voluntarily re-established [themselves] in the country which [they] left or outside which [they] remained owing to fear of persecution."[32]

Those who "can no longer, because the circumstances in connection with which [they have] been recognized as a refugee have ceased to exist, continue to refuse to avail [themselves] of the protection of the country of [their] nationality; provided that this paragraph shall not apply to a refugee falling under section A (1) of [Article I] who [are] able to invoke compelling reasons arising out of previous persecution for refusing to avail [themselves] of the protection of the country of nationality."[33]

---

[29] Refugee Convention, Article I(C)(1)
[30] *Ibid.*, Article I(C)(2)
[31] *Ibid.*, I(C)(3)
[32] *Ibid.*, I(C)(4)
[33] Ibid., I(C)(5)

And those "who [have] no nationality...because the circumstances in connection with which [they have] been recognized as a refugee have ceased to exist, are able to return to the country of [their] former habitual residence...."[34]

In 2009, Article I of Refugee Convention applied to Burundi, Liberia, and Rwanda with respect to sections (C)(5) and (C)(6): "Canada will lift a ban on deporting illegal immigrants to Burundi, Liberia and Rwanda after an internal review showed 'improved conditions' in those countries."[35]

There are three types of Removal Orders issued by IRCC or CBSA. These are Departure Orders, Exclusion Orders and Deportation Orders.[36] With a Departure Order, one must leave Canada within 30 days after the order takes effect. An Exclusion Order bars one from returning to Canada for one year. A Departure Order automatically becomes a Deportation Order if one fails to leave Canada and it is permanent unless an application for Authorization to Return to Canada (ARC) is granted.

In November 2022, the United Nations issued a deportation ban on Congo DR from certain parts of the country:

---

[34] Ibid., I(C)(6)

[35] *CBC News*, "Deportation ban lifted for 3 African countries," July 24th, 2009.

[36] CBSA, "Removal from Canada," https://www.cbsa-asfc.gc.ca/security-securite/rem-ren-eng.html, accessed on October 12th, 2023.

UNHCR, the UN Refugee Agency, has released today an updated return advisory for the Democratic Republic of the Congo (DRC), reiterating its call for a ban on forced returns, including of asylum-seekers who have had their claims rejected, to the eastern provinces of North Kivu, South Kivu, and Ituri. UNHCR also calls on States to grant refugees access to their territory and treat them in accordance with the 1969 OAU Convention Governing the Specific Aspects of Refugee Problems in Africa, and the 1951 Convention Relating to the Status of Refugees.[37]

In certain exceptional circumstances as the one above, the United Nations High Commission for Refugees (UNHCR) may issue such bans. These bans are issued where civilians' lives and displaced people are at risk of being attacked. The case of Congo DR meets that criterion.

---

[37] "UN Refugee Agency calls for ban on forced returns of asylum-seekers to eastern DR Congo," < https://www.unhcr.org/news/briefing-notes/un-refugee-agency-calls-ban-forced-returns-asylum-seekers-eastern-dr-congo> accessed on October 9th, 2023.

3 | STATUTORY DEFINITION OF A REFUGEE

> In Canada, a claimant can be accepted as a Convention refugee or as a protected person or both.

Section 96 and subsection 97(1) of *Immigration and Refugee Protection Act* (IRPA)[38] define a **Convention refugee** (CR) as a person in need of protection:

Convention Refugee

96 A Convention refugee is a person who, by reason of a well-founded fear of persecution for reasons of race, religion, nationality, membership in a particular social group or political opinion,

---

[38] S.C. 2001, c. 27

(a) is outside each of their countries of nationality and is unable or, by reason of that fear, unwilling to avail themself of the protection of each of those countries; or

(b) not having a country of nationality, is outside the country of their former habitual residence and is unable or, by reason of that fear, unwilling to return to that country.

Person in Need of Protection

97 (1) A person in need of protection is a person in Canada whose removal to their country or countries of nationality or, if they do not have a country of nationality, their country of former habitual residence, would subject them personally

(a) to a danger, believed on substantial grounds to exist, of torture within the meaning of Article 1 of the Convention Against Torture; or

(b) to a risk to their life or to a risk of cruel and unusual treatment or punishment if

(i) the person is unable or, because of that risk, unwilling to avail themself of the protection of that country,

(ii) the risk would be faced by the person in every part of that country and is not faced generally by other individuals in or from that country,

(iii) the risk is not inherent or incidental to lawful sanctions, unless imposed in disregard of accepted international standards, and

(iv) the risk is not caused by the inability of that country to provide adequate health or medical care.

(2) A person in Canada who is a member of a class of persons prescribed by the regulations as being in need of protection is also a person in need of protection.

Trite Law and Procedure

In Canada, conferring of refugee status or protection is a **trite law**.[39] This means that one ought only to meet the requirement of s. 96 or ss. 97(1) of IRPA. It is common practice in Canadian refugee law that one is usually found under both sections.

As noted, section 96 and subsection 97(1) of IRPA are uprooted directly from the UN Refugee Convention. A refugee is only so by virtue of the convention. Thus, refugees coming before the IRB under the authority of IRPA, are, in fact, coming under the protection of the UN Refugee Convention. They become CRs when they successfully defend their claims at the RPD.

---

[39] A principle of law so notorious and entrenched that it is commonly known and rarely disputed. See Trite Law Definition < http://www.duhaime.org/LegalDictionary/T/TriteLaw.aspx> (Accessed on November 24th, 2019)

A refugee is, thus, a person who has a **founded fear of persecution** in their country of citizenship or of former habitual residence. This fear must both be **subjective** (it affects them personally) and **objective** (the State conditions make persecution possible). To make a refugee claim in Canada, the **Claimant** (the person making a refugee claim) must have *left* their own country and must be within Canada.[40] The claim can be made at two points.

The claim can be made at the **Point of Entry (POE)** either at the airport or the border, depending on where the claimant first enters Canada. This applies to those who are seeking asylum[41] straight upon arrival in Canada, and mostly it concerns those who have no lawful right or authorization to enter Canada. Those who make claims at the POE are briefly detained by the CBSA officers.

---

[40] This injunction (namely, being out of your country) applies to refugee resettlement programs under the United Nations High Commissioner for Refugees (UNHCR) as well; the Claimant must be out of their countries of citizenship in order to apply to be refugees in Canada. Such a person will become a Government-Assisted Refugee (or "GAR"), defined as a person who is outside Canada and has been determined to be a Convention rrefugee and who receives financial and other support from the Government of Canada or Province of Quebec for up to one year after their arrival in Canada. GARs are selected from applicants referred by the UNHCR and other referral organizations.

[41] Amesty International defines an **asylum seeker** as "a person who has left their country and is seeking protection from persecution and serious human rights violations in another country, but who has not yet been legally recognized as a refugee and is waiting to receive a decision on their asylum claim." A **refugee** seems to indicate a person who is an asylum seeker or whose decision has already been made to become a refugee.

They are detained (arrested) because they are inadmissible to Canada. If they decide or show intention to make a refugee claim, they will be issued with removal orders subject to appearing before an adjudicator at the IRB. At this point, these people are neither refugee claimants nor refugees; they are considered **Foreign Nationals** (a Foreign National is legally defined in Canadian as "a person who is not a Canadian citizen or a permanent resident, and includes a stateless person"[42]) who must be subjected to **examination** by a CBSA officer who may recommend a hearing at the ID.

If the foreign national does not show any intention to claim for refugee protection in Canada, a CBSA officer may refer the matter to the ID for an **Admissibility Hearing.**[43] An admissibility hearing may also be conducted for those refugee claimants who, for one reason or the other, failed to appear for their hearing and must be examined before they are removed from Canada.

---

[42] IRPA, s. 2(1); also see, Glossary, "Foreign National," < https://www.canada.ca/en/services/immigration-citizenship/helpcentre/glossary.html> (accessed on July 10th, 2020)
[43] An admissibility hearing may be held pursuant to sections 44 and 45 of IRPA to decide if one is allowed to come into or stay in Canada. It applies to both permanent residents and foreign nationals. Admissibility hearings can be started for any of these reasons: Criminal convictions; human or international rights violations; risk to security in Canada; health reasons; financial reasons; misrepresentation or not being truthful in immigration applications; or failure to comply with IRPA. It also applies to minor children (children 16 years and below) who have travelled alone to Canada.

If the foreign national indicates that they would like to make a refugee claim, the CBSA officer will refer them to an in-land reporting center to make a refugee claim by submitting the prescribed forms within fifteen (15) days. The claim can also be made *within* Canada. This applies to all those who came to Canada with lawful authorization (Visas) and who subsequently made a refugee claim in Canada. These must report themselves to the **In-Land Reporting Center** and make a claim there.

In-land reporting is a two-step process. First, the foreign national must attend at the center with the following documents and forms: All identity documents, such as passports, birth certificates, national identity documents or any such documents. The foreign national must also take to the center completed immigration and refugee forms, including the following immigration forms: Generic and Schedule A – Background Declaration.

The foreign national should also complete the following refugee forms: **Basis of Claim** or **BOC** form (formerly the Personal Information Form or **PIF**) with the narrative attached thereto, and Schedule 12.[44] The BOC form is a very important refugee claim form. The foreign national must also take four (4) passport-photos, and a checklist.

---

[44] Post-Covid-19 has eliminated the completion of Schedule 12. Information that was required in this schedule can now be solicited through a refugee portal summary.

The IRCC officers at the center will review the BOC narrative and forms and the immigration forms and ascertain that the person has met the criteria for making a refugee claim in Canada. Recently, the IRCC introduced an Integrated Claim Analysis Center (ICAC) Checklist to assist the IRB-RPD to streamline document collection.[45] Once that has been satisfied, the officer will arrange for an **Interview**.

The purpose of the interview is to determine whether there are any issues, usually security in nature or otherwise that might not qualify the foreign national to making a successful refugee claim in Canada. The officers will also review the foreign national's previous immigration history to make sure that the person is credible or otherwise has misrepresented. Depending on the outcome, the person will be provided with a document called **Refugee Protection Claimant's Document**[46] or RPCD, which technically entitles the "claimant" to the Rule of Natural Justice or the Right to be Heard (or due process of law).

Even if credibility or misrepresentation issues have been discovered by the officers, the claimant will still be entitled to procedural fairness so that the claimant can defend the claim and allegations of misrepresentation. Whether the Minister has elected to **Intervene** or not, the matter will now be referred to the RPD for adjudication.

---

[45] See Appendix V for a redacted sample. This author was one of the first whose clients used this system.
[46] Nigerians refer to this document as "Brown Paper."

(Ministerial Intervention means that the Minister of Immigration will be opposing the refugee claim on the basis of credibility findings or other grounds). The **Minister's Counsel**, as the Minister's representative is referred to, may intervene directly by appearing at the hearing or may only make written submissions without attending at the hearing.

A claimant is further entitled to some limited access to social, health and employment privileges while she waits for her hearing in Canada. The **Notice to Appear for a Hearing**, which is a notice provided to the claimant to appear before an adjudicator to defend the claim, may be given to the claimant at the Interview or may be mailed later to the claimant at the address provided in the Generic and the BOC forms. It is important that the claimant notifies the RPD whenever there is a change of address in order not to miss the hearing.

The limited social, health and employment needs the claimant is entitled to at this stage are the requirement to attend at a Panel Physician's office and undergo medical examination. A **Panel Physician**, formerly Designated Medical Doctor, is an IRCC-appointed or designated medical doctor who can perform medical tests and send results directly to IRCC. IRCC does not accept the medical results of any other doctors. Other entitlements are Work Permit, Social Welfare, if needed, and health coverage. Note that the federal government will automatically cover the medical needs of the claimants for first few months under the **Interim Federal Health Program (IFHP)**.

The IFHP, "Provides within Canada, limited, temporary coverage of health-care benefits to resettled refugees, refugee claimants, and certain others who are not eligible for provincial or territorial health insurance."[47] Health Insurance is defined as, "A Canadian provincial or territorial government program that pays for essential health services provided by doctors, hospitals and certain non-physician practitioners. Newcomers must apply to their provincial or territorial health insurance plan to get coverage and a health card."[48]

Afterwards, the provincial health system will kick in, depending on the health insurance plan that exists in the province in which the refugee claim was made. For example, if the claim was made in Ontario Province, the province's **Ontario Health Insurance Plan** or **OHIP** will subsequently cover the claimant.[49]

---

[47] "Interim Federal Health Program Policy," < https://www.canada.ca/en/immigration-refugees-citizenship/corporate/mandate/policies-operational-instructions-agreements/interim-federal-health-program-policy.html> (accessed on November 22nd, 2019)

[48] "Health Insurance," Glossary, *supra*.

[49] For more details on OHIP, see, "Apply for OHIP and get a health card," < https://www.ontario.ca/page/apply-ohip-and-get-health-card#section-0> (accessed on November 22nd, 2019)

The RPD will provide two dates, one is the actual date of hearing or the **Notice to Appear**, and the other is reserved for those who may miss the hearing (Show-Cause). The Show-Cause date is not the date for the second chance for those who failed to appear; it is, rather, a date to meet the adjudicator and explain the reasons for failure to appear and whether another hearing should be scheduled. The IRB explains it this way:[50]

> The RPD will send you a Notice to Appear by mail when your claim is ready to be heard. On the Notice to Appear, there are two dates. The first date is the date of your hearing. The second date in your Notice to Appear is for a special hearing. In the event that you do not attend your hearing, you must appear at your special hearing to explain why you were not able to attend your hearing. At the special hearing, the member will determine whether your claim should be declared abandoned.
>
> Hearings usually take half a day and take place in private in order to protect you and your family. There is usually a short break about halfway through the hearing.

---

[50] IRB, "Claiming refugee protection - 4. Attending your hearing," < https://irb-cisr.gc.ca/en/applying-refugee-protection/Pages/index4.aspx> (accessed on April 29th, 2020)

Young children under the age of 12 who are accompanied by an adult making a refugee claim are not required to appear before the Refugee Protection Division unless the presiding member requires their attendance. When a member determines that it is necessary for a young Claimant to attend the hearing, you will be informed at the earliest possible opportunity. In some situations, older children will need to participate in the hearing. If you have concerns or questions about your child participating in the hearing, contact the RPD before your hearing or raise your concerns with the member at the hearing. If the RPD member cannot be in the same city as you, your hearing may take place by videoconference.

It is important to notify counsel way in advance if the claimant will not attend the hearing on the date scheduled. Counsel then may make an **application** for a change of hearing date or for an adjournment. As long as this requisition does not prejudice the Minister, is made for a legitimate reason and in good faith and in good time, the Refugee Protection Division (RPD) may consider changing the hearing date to an earliest available future date.

To be granted a refugee status, a claimant must prove, on a balance of probabilities, that they meet the definition of a refugee or protected person pursuant to section 96 and subsection 97(1) of IRPA. The **Balance of Probabilities** is a legal standard of proof required to prove that the person is a refugee.

The standard is lower than the criminal law threshold which requires the Crown (the Government) to prove a case **Beyond a Reasonable Doubt**, that is, to only convict an accused where it is very certain that they had committed a crime charged. Therefore, the Board's Member will grant refugee status to a claimant who, on the balance of probabilities (or the preponderance of evidence), proves or establishes that they are more probable than not to be subjected to persecution if they returned to their country of citizenship or former habitual residence. If it was a scale of 100 percent, the claimant would succeed in making a refugee claim if they only established about 51 percent.[51]

In subsequent chapters, we will discuss how the claimant establishes, on the balance of probabilities, that they are a refugee or a person in need of protection in Canada. The BOC will be discussed in great details. It is assumed that the BOC, with its attendant schedule, if applicable, has been completed with the requirement of country-specific condition in place. In this book, Nigeria is the country of focus.

---

[51] However, as shall be discussed in Chapter 3, under the Refugee Determination System in Canada, one needs not to establish on the balance of probability to succeed in a refugee claim; one just needs to have a good reason to win. See *Adjei test* in *Joseph Adjei v. Minister of Employment and Immigration,* R.S.C. 1976, C. 52

4 | BASIS OF CLAIM

In Canada, a claimant must complete a form
called Basis of Claim (BOC), formerly,
Personal Identification Form (PIF), and
provide a written, dated and signed narrative
or story they intend to rely upon at the
hearing. The form and narrative may
collectively be referred to as Basis of Claim
(BOC) as well.

Basis of Claim

Basis of Claim or BOC is, arguably, the most important document so far as a refugee claim is concerned. It is the basis or the notable information the claimant provides as the basis of their refugee claim. This information, subject to amendment before the hearing, if necessary, becomes the claimant's record in the Canadian immigration database. It cannot be easily changed afterwards without inviting allegations of misrepresentation.

The BOC narrative must be thought-through wisely, cogently and accurately.[52] No refugee claim has been successful without a well-written and presented BOC narrative or simply, the "Story." The story must accurately identify the claimant, including their legal names, dates of birth, country of origin or citizenship, marital status, number of children, if any – this should include their names, ages and marital statuses and so on – educational levels, academic designation or qualification, if applicable, and any pertinent identifying information necessary to establishing a credible claim.

The BOC story must show a relationship between the State and the alleged persecution. Canada cannot protect people who are not in danger of their own governments. Canada is a signatory to international conventions, but Canada will be declaring war with another sovereign State if it arbitrarily attempts to protect nationals from other sovereign States.

In Canada, there is no bifurcation of claims. Dual citizens must be in danger in both countries to be protected in Canada. The 2004 Third Safe Country agreement bars one from making a refugee claim if entering through the Canada–US land border. On-transit claimants, family members or unaccompanied minors, etc., are exempted.[53]

---

[52] See Appendix I, Sample redacted BOC narratives.
[53] See *Canadian Council for Refugees v. Canada (Citizenship and Immigration)*, 2023 SCC 17.

The basis for protection is the assumption that the claimant is either stateless or their own country and government cannot protect them, directly or indirectly. Only state actors and agents can truly persecute the foreign national under the law. However, other non-state actors can be agents of persecution, such as abusive spouses, organized criminal rings, cultural or customary or clan groups, terrorist gangs, etc.

The Meaning of Credibility in Refugee Law

Most, if not, all, refugee claims are won and lost on credibility. Evidence is essential. However, one should look at it from this point of view: How can a total stranger who happens to be hearing the claim believe for certain in your story? How should a Member believe if you are telling the truth or not? The simple answer is **Credibility**.

Board Members are humans. They cannot know what happened to the claimant just by intuition or guessing. The only thing they have, usually, is the BOC story, the National Documentation Package (NDP), and the evidence submitted, if any, with the claim. They expect that the claimant's testimony will be consistent with the BOC story submitted.

Credibility is synonymous with **believability**. It is the quality of being trusted and believed. And in relation to the witness' testimony (*viva voce*), credibility relates to the testimony of a witness during a hearing. There are generally five bases for credibility.

First, to be found credible, the claimant must be trusted. Trust can be illusive in refugee hearing but particular attention to what the claimant says, how they appear, their voice projection and general demeanor, can go a long way in establishing trust with the adjudicator.

Trust is earned. It follows that the claimant should pay attention to their choice of words, how polite, respectful or careful they are with their general presentation. Once the adjudicator believes and observes that the claimant is whole and upright, and, therefore, candid with overall presentation, the adjudicator will trust the claimant. Trust is also earned when the claimant pays particular attention to procedural matters, such as filing the evidence in good time, making necessary changes to the BOC story before the hearing,[54] and making necessary applications in good time and in good faith.

Amendments to the BOC form or narrative made in good time and in good faith are accepted by the RPD.

---

[54] At least more than ten days before the hearing, if necessary.

Second, credibility is built up through the reliability of what the claimant says. Reliability means the truthfulness of what is said which is manifested through accuracy and exactitude of the statements made. Reliability is the accuracy of the testimony. It is one's ability to answer questions truthfully and accurately.

Only the adjudicator and counsel, if represented, will have access to the BOC narrative. The claimant will not have access to the BOC narrative at the hearing but will be expected to answer questions according to the BOC narrative. The claimant cannot deviate from the story or make arbitrary changes to the original story in the process.

She must keep the same tenor and sequence of the story. To be reliable, the claimant should remember names, places, dates and important landmarks in the story. It should be emphasized that reliability, and thus, credibility, will be impeached where the claimant is forgetful or negligent in answering questions asked, or is inconsistent with the submitted BOC narrative.

Third, the logical flow of the claimant's testimony establishes credibility. The story must have a logical trajectory – each paragraph connecting the next in a logical and seamless flow of ideas and sense. The story should have a sensible start, middle and ending.

Fourth, it is the sincerity and personal credibility of the testimony that establish credibility. The message and the medium are the same. The person telling the story cannot be separated from the story. It is, therefore, important that the witness establishes personal credibility by the way they tell their story and answer questions. Generally, the claimant (witness) must do the following three things:

(a) They must only answer the questions being asked. Failure to follow this rule may force the adjudicator to draw a negative inference , and this might damage credibility beyond repair. If answering through an interpreter, it is vital to keep answers short.

(b) State so if they do not understand the question or ask the adjudicator to restate or rephrase the question; and

(c) Say so if they do not know or cannot remember the answer. It is better to not answer a question one does not know or cannot remember than to guess or answer a question one does not know. Credibility means that one is able to say they do not know if they do not know.

Fifth and last, the refugee hearing process is an **inquisitorial process**. This means that the adjudicator conducts the hearing like an inquiry. The hearing only becomes **adversarial** when the Minister decides to intervene. Otherwise, both the claimant and her counsel must be prepared to follow the guideline and process as determined by the adjudicator.

The adjudicator sets the tone and trajectory of how the hearing is to be conducted. All that both the claimant and counsel should do is to be prepared. Because the IRB sets the direction of how the hearing should be conducted, the adjudicator has freedom (or **discretion**) and ample opportunity to observe both how the claimant answers questions and how she behaves during the hearing. This is called observing the **personal demeanor** and **emotional disposition** of the witness (claimant). This will generally involve the following three aspects:

(a) How and what the claimant wears. It is always better to be dressed modestly and avoid both over- and underdressing. The best precaution is to error on the side of decency and morality, rather than being overtly extravagant or casual. The claimant must observe basic hygiene, dress modestly, comb hair well and wear clothes that are well-pressed and in good taste. It is advisable to avoid outrageous colors – navy blue, black, dark grey suites or pants

are ideal for men. For woman, closed
shoes, long dresses or skirts and less tight
clothing are suitable. Both men and
women should avoid wearing expensive
jewelry and heavily-scented perfumes.[55]

(b) Eye contact with the adjudicator;

(c) And a strong voice that can be heard but
that is not excessive and irritating to the
adjudicator. If there is an interpreter, the
claimant (witness) should speak in short
sentences and allow the interpreter to
finish the interpretation before saying
another word. It is good policy to allow
the interpreter to finish talking before the
witness can say another word. It is equally
important to allow the adjudicator to finish
the sentence before the witness can
answer. Speaking through the microphone
with a firm voice is also suitable for the
purposes of recording. The microphone
only picks the claimant's voice. It does not
record the claimant's demeanor, non-
verbal gestures, etc.

---

[55] Most Boards and Courts in Ontario facilitate a scent-free
atmosphere.

In the next chapters, we will provide a compilation of case law, policy, judicial determinations and jurisprudence already prepared by the IRB. The aim of the ensuing chapters, therefore, is to expose the claimant to ready materials and reasonings of the IRB so that the claimant is prepared to defend the claim. The materials, for the most part, have been uprooted in their entirety and only minimal modifications and changes have been made, and only for relevance, emphasis and contextual analysis.

Important information on Nigeria is weaved through to provide the claimant with enough preparatory materials. All the cases, materials and information collected in this book are meant to grant a Nigerian refugee claimant the opportunity to ace credibility issues on their refugee claims in Canada.

5 | IMPORTANT FACTS ABOUT NIGERIA

In 2022, about 1,581 Nigerian claims were referred to the RPD. Of these, about 1,315 claims were accepted and around 728 were rejected. There were about 22 abandoned claims, and 666 claims were withdrawn.

Map of Nigeria

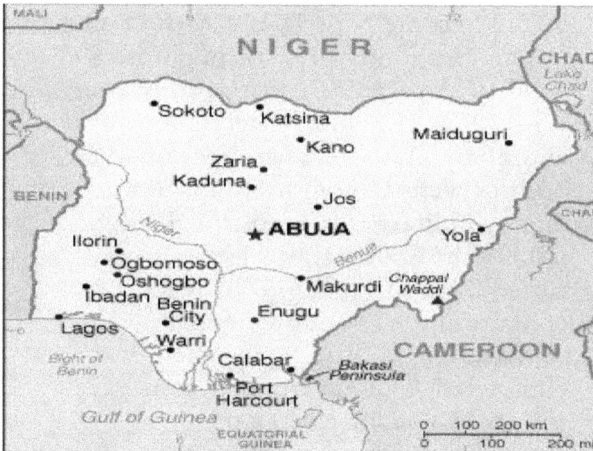

(Source: World Fact Book)[56]

---

[56]World Fact Book
https://www.cia.gov/library/publications/resources/the-world-factbook/geos/ni.html> (accessed on August 28th, 2020)

Nigeria Up Close

Nigeria is named after the Niger River that flows through the west of the country to the Atlantic Ocean; from a native term "Ni Gir" meaning "River Gir." Nigeria was colonized by Britain and attained its independence on October 1st, 1960. After independence, Nigeria was buffeted by coups and military governments. Civilian rule effectively started in 1999 with the authorship of a new constitution. Corruption and political instability continue to dog Nigeria, which relies heavily on a petroleum economy. World Fact book captures the genesis and continuity of Nigeria in this fashion:

> British influence and control over what would become Nigeria and Africa's most populous country grew through the 19th century. A series of constitutions after World War II granted Nigeria greater autonomy. After independence in 1960, politics were marked by coups and mostly military rule, until the death of a military head of state in 1998 allowed for a political transition. In 1999, a new constitution was adopted and a peaceful transition to civilian government was completed. The government continues to face the daunting task of institutionalizing democracy and reforming a petroleum-based economy, whose revenues have been squandered through decades of corruption and mismanagement.

In addition, Nigeria continues to experience longstanding ethnic and religious tensions. Although both the 2003 and 2007 presidential elections were marred by significant irregularities and violence, Nigeria is currently experiencing its longest period of civilian rule since independence. The general elections of 2007 marked the first civilian-to-civilian transfer of power in the country's history. National and state elections in 2011 and 2015 were generally regarded as credible. The 2015 election was also heralded for the fact that the then-umbrella opposition party, the All Progressives Congress, defeated the long-ruling People's Democratic Party that had governed since 1999, and assumed the presidency, marking the first peaceful transfer of power from one party to another. Presidential and legislative elections were held in early 2019 and deemed broadly free and fair despite voting irregularities, intimidation, and violence.[57]

Nigeria is found in Western Africa, bordering the Gulf of Guinea, between Benin and Cameroon. Nigeria bears geographical coordinates of 10 00 N, 8 00 E. It has a total land area of 923,768 sq. km, land mass of 910,768 sq. km and about 13,000 sq. km is covered with water.

---

[57] *Ibid.*

Nigeria's land boundary is about 4,477 km. and with a coastline of about 853 km. In terms of climate, Nigeria is varying mostly among equatorial in the south, tropical in the center, and arid in the north. Its terrain includes southern lowlands merging into central hills and plateaus, mountains in southeast, and plains in north. Nigeria's mean elevation is at 380 m, lowest point at the Atlantic Ocean of 0 m, and the highest point at Chappal Waddi of about 2,419 m.[58]

In terms of land use, Nigeria is about 78 percent (2011 est.) agricultural land, about 37.3 percent (2011 est.) / permanent crops of arable land, about 7.4 percent (2011 est.) / permanent pasture, 33.3 percent (2011 est.) is forest: 9.5 percent (2011 est.) and the rest of 12.5 percent (2011 est.) is other. Nigeria depends mostly on irrigation, which is about 2,930 sq. km (2012).

The population of Nigeria is distributed as follows: It has the largest population of any African nation; significant population clusters are scattered throughout the country, with the highest density areas being in the south and southwest.[59]

---

[58] *Ibid.*
[59] *Ibid.*

As of July 2020, the population of Nigeria stood at 214,028,302.[60]

The Niger River enters the country in the northwest and flows southward through tropical rain forests and swamps to its delta in the Gulf of Guinea.[61]

In terms of ethnicity, the following is notable: Hausas account for 30 percent; Yoruba 15.5 percent; Igbo (Ibo) 15.2 percent; Fulani 6 percent; Tiv 2.4 percent; Kanuri/Beriberi 2.4 percent; Ibibio 1.8 percent; Ijaw/Izon 1.8 percent; and others about 24.7 percent, according to the 2018 estimates.[62]

Notable languages include English (official), Hausa, Yoruba, Igbo (Ibo), Fulani, and over 500 additional indigenous languages.

Nigeria is Africa's most populous country, composing of more than 250 ethnic groups. Religious groups are distributed as follows: Muslim 53.5 percent; Roman Catholics 10.6 percent; other Christians (mostly Protestants) 35.3 percent; and others, about 0.6 percent, according to the 2018 estimates.[63]

---

[60] Estimates for Nigeria explicitly consider the effects of excess mortality due to AIDS; this can result in lower life expectancy, higher infant mortality, higher death rates, lower population growth rates, and changes in the distribution of population by age and sex than would otherwise be expected (see *ibid* footnote)

[61] *Ibid.*

[62] World Fact Book, *supra.*

[63] *Ibid.*

In terms of Nigeria's demography, the following is notable:

> Nigeria's population is projected to grow from more than 186 million people in 2016 to 392 million in 2050, becoming the world's fourth most populous country. Nigeria's sustained high population growth rate will continue for the foreseeable future because of population momentum and its high birth rate. Abuja has not successfully implemented family planning programs to reduce and space births because of a lack of political will, government financing, and the availability and affordability of services and products, as well as a cultural preference for large families. Increased educational attainment, especially among women, and improvements in health care are needed to encourage and to better enable parents to opt for smaller families.

Nigeria needs to harness the potential of its burgeoning youth population in order to boost economic development, reduce widespread poverty, and channel large numbers of unemployed youth into productive activities and away from ongoing religious and ethnic violence. While most movement of Nigerians is internal, significant emigration regionally and to the West provides an outlet for Nigerians looking for economic opportunities, seeking asylum, and increasingly pursuing higher education. Immigration largely of West Africans continues to be insufficient to offset emigration and the loss of highly skilled workers. Nigeria also is a major source, transit, and destination country for forced labor and sex trafficking.[64]

---

[64] *Ibid.*

Nigeria's population growth rate is about 2.53 percent.[65] Its birth rate is about 34.6 births/1,000 population.[66] Its death rate is about 9.1 deaths/1,000 population.[67] Its maternity rate is at 917 deaths/100,000 live births.[68] Its infant mortality rate is at 59.8 deaths/1,000 live births. Life expectancy at birth is at 60.4 years (male: 58.6 years; and female: 62.3 years).[69] Total fertility rate is at 4.72 children born/woman,[70] and contraceptive prevalence rate is at 27.6 percent.[71] Physician density is at 0.45 physicians/1,000 population.[72] HIV/AIDS - adult prevalence rate is at 1.5 percent,[73] HIV/AIDS - people living with HIV/AIDS is estimated at 1.9 million,[74] and the number of people who have died with HIV/AIDS is around 53,200.[75] And its migration rate is about -0.2 migrant(s)/1,000 population.[76]

---

[65] 2020 est.
[66] 2020 est.
[67] 2020 est.
[68] 2017 est.
[69] 2020 est.
[70] 2020 est.
[71] As of 2018
[72] As of 2016
[73] 2018 est.
[74] As of 2018
[75] 2017 est.
[76] 2020 est.

Nigeria's population distribution is as follows: It has the largest population of any African nation, with significant population clusters scattered throughout the country; the highest density areas being in the south and southwest.[77]

In terms of diseases:

> On 7 October 2019, the Centers for Disease Control and Prevention issued a Travel Health Notice for a Yellow Fever outbreak in Nigeria; a large, ongoing outbreak of yellow fever in Nigeria began in September 2017; the outbreak is now spread throughout the country with the Nigerian Ministry of Health reporting cases of the disease in all 36 states and the Federal Capital Territory; the CDC recommends travelers going to Nigeria should receive vaccination against yellow fever at least 10 days before travel and should take steps to prevent mosquito bites while there; those never vaccinated against yellow fever should avoid travel to Nigeria during the outbreak. Widespread ongoing transmission of a respiratory illness caused by the novel coronavirus (COVID-19) is occurring throughout Nigeria; as of 19 August 2020, Nigeria has reported 49,895 confirmed cases of COVID-19 with 981 deaths; as of 19 March 2020, the Government of Nigeria has restricted entry into Nigeria for travelers from the following high incidence countries: China, Italy, Iran, Norway, South Korea, Spain, Japan, France, Germany, US, UK, Netherlands, and Switzerland.[78]

---

[77] World Fact Book, *supra.*
[78] See World fact Book, *supra.*

Nigeria is heavily urbanized, with about 52 percent of total population living in urbans.[79] In terms of literacy, about 62 percent of people aged 15 years and over can read and write.[80] Unemployment among the youth aged between 15 years and 24 years is at about 13.8 percent as of 2016.

In political terms, Nigeria has a federal type of government. Nigeria is a federal presidential republic, with its capital City at Abuja. "Abuja is a planned capital city, it replaced Lagos in 1991; situated in the center of the country, Abuja takes its name from a nearby town, now renamed Suleja."[81]

Nigeria has 36 states and one territory: Abia, Adamawa, Akwa Ibom, Anambra, Bauchi, Bayelsa, Benue, Borno, Cross River, Delta, Ebonyi, Edo, Ekiti, Enugu, Federal Capital Territory, Gombe, Imo, Jigawa, Kaduna, Kano, Katsina, Kebbi, Kogi, Kwara, Lagos, Nasarawa, Niger, Ogun, Ondo, Osun, Oyo, Plateau, Rivers, Sokoto, Taraba, Yobe, and Zamfara.

Nigeria has a mixed legal system of English common law, Islamic law (in 12 northern states), and traditional law. Nigeria endorses a dual citizenship arrangement; at least one parent must be a citizen of Nigeria.

---

[79] As of 2020
[80] Of these, about 71.3 percent are male and about 52.7 percent are female accruing to the estimates compiled in 2018.
[81] World fact Book, *supra.*

In terms of naturalization, one has to be resident in Nigeria for 15 years to be a citizen. The president of Nigeria is the chief of state, head of government, and commander-in-chief of the armed forces.

The cabinet is Federal Executive Council appointed by the president but constrained constitutionally to include at least one member from each of the 36 states.[82]

The president is directly elected by qualified majority popular vote and at least 25 percent of the votes cast in 24 of Nigeria's 36 states; the president is elected for a 4-year term (eligible for a second term); elections were held on February 25th, 2023, in which Bola Ahmed Adekunle Tinubu emerged the winner.

Nigeria has a bicameral legislation; a bicameral National Assembly consisting of: Senate (109 seats - 3 each for the 36 states and 1 for Abuja-Federal Capital Territory; members are directly elected in single-seat constituencies by simple majority vote to serve 4-year terms).[83] The House of Representatives (360 seats; members are directly elected in single-seat constituencies by simple majority vote to serve 4-year terms).

[82] *Ibid.*
[83] *Ibid.*

The judicial branch consists of the Supreme Court (which consists of the Chief Justice and 15 justices). Judge are selected or appointed by the president upon the recommendation of the National Judicial Council, a 23-member independent body of federal and state judicial officials.

Judge appointments are confirmed by the Senate; judges serve until age 70 in subordinate courts. The Court of Appeal, the Federal High Court, the High Court of the Federal Capital Territory, the Sharia Court of Appeal of the Federal Capital Territory, the Customary Court of Appeal of the Federal Capital Territory, and the state court system similar in structure to federal system, make up the court system in Nigeria.

As of 2020, the following political parties existed in Nigeria: Accord Party or ACC [Mohammad Lawal Malado]; All Progressives Congress or APC [Adams Oshiomhole]; All Progressives Grand Alliance or APGA [Victor Ike Oye]; Democratic Peoples Party or DPP [Biodun Ogunbiyi]; Labor Party or LP [Alhai Abdulkadir Abdulsalam]; Peoples Democratic Party or PDP [Uche Secondus]; and Young Progressive Party or YPP [Kingsley Moghalu].

The national symbols of Nigeria are: The eagle and national colors of green and white.

The flag is described as follows: Three equal vertical bands of green (hoist side), white, and green; the color green represents the forests and abundant natural wealth of the country, and the color white stands for peace and unity of the nation.

Nigeria's National Anthem is a generally patriotic musical composition - usually in the form of a song or hymn of praise - that evokes and eulogizes the history, traditions, or struggles of a nation or its people.

The National Anthem can be officially recognized as a national song by a country's constitution or by an enacted law, or simply by tradition.

Although most anthems contain lyrics, some do not. The National Anthem of Nigeria is: "Arise Oh Compatriots, Nigeria's Call Obey."

The National Anthem was adopted by John A. Ilechukwu, Eme Etim Akpan, B.A. Ogunnaike, Sotu Omoigui, P.O. Aderibigbe, and Benedict Elide Odiase in 1978. The lyrics were a mixture of the five top entries in a national contest of that year.

Nigeria's economy may be summarized as:

Nigeria is Sub Saharan Africa's largest economy and relies heavily on oil as its main source of foreign exchange earnings and government revenues. Following the 2008-09 global financial crises, the banking sector was effectively re-capitalized, and regulation enhanced. Since then, Nigeria's economic growth has been driven by growth in agriculture, telecommunications, and services. Economic diversification and strong growth have not translated into a significant decline in poverty levels....

Despite its strong fundamentals, oil-rich Nigeria has been hobbled by inadequate power supply, lack of infrastructure, delays in the passage of legislative reforms, an inefficient property registration system, restrictive trade policies, an inconsistent regulatory environment, a slow and ineffective judicial system, unreliable dispute resolution mechanisms, insecurity, and pervasive corruption. Regulatory constraints and security risks have limited new investment in oil and natural gas, and Nigeria's oil production had been contracting every year since 2012 until a slight rebound in 2017.

President BUHARI, elected in March 2015, ha[d] established a cabinet of economic ministers that include[d] several technocrats, and he ha[d] announced plans to increase transparency, diversify the economy away from oil, and improve fiscal management, but ha[d] taken a primarily protectionist approach that favor[ed] domestic producers at the expense of consumers. President BUHARI ran on an anti-corruption platform, and ha[d] made some headway in alleviating corruption, such as implementation of a Treasury Single Account that allow[ed] the government to better manage its resources and a more transparent government payroll and personnel system that eliminated duplicate and "ghost workers." The government [was] also working to develop stronger public-private partnerships for roads, agriculture, and power.

Nigeria entered recession in 2016 as a result of lower oil prices and production, exacerbated by militant attacks on oil and gas infrastructure in the Niger Delta region, coupled with detrimental economic policies, including foreign exchange restrictions. GDP growth turned positive in 2017 as oil prices recovered and output stabilized.

In Nigeria, 40.1 percent of people are poor according to the 2018/19 national monetary poverty line, and 63 percent are multidimensionally poor according to the National MPI 2022. Multidimensional poverty is higher in rural areas, where 72 percent of people are poor, compared to 42 percent of people in urban areas.[84]

The Nigeria's purchasing power parity (PPP)[85] stood at: US$1.121 trillion,[86] US$1.112 trillion,[87] and US$1.13 trillion.[88]

Gross Domestic Product (GDP) *per* capita[89] in Nigeria was: US$5,900,[90] US$6,100,[91] and Us$6,300.[92]

---

[84] National Bureau of Statistics, "Nigeria launches its most extensive national measure of multidimensional poverty," November 17th, 2022.

[85] This entry gives the gross domestic product (GDP) or value of all final goods and services produced within a nation in a given year. A nation's GDP at purchasing power parity (PPP) exchange rates is the sum value of all goods and services produced in the country valued at prices prevailing in the United States in the year noted. This is the measure most economists prefer when looking at per-capita welfare and when comparing living conditions or use of resources across countries.

[86] 2017 est.

[87] 2016 est.

[88] 2015 est.

[89] This entry shows GDP on a purchasing power parity basis divided by population as of 1 July for the same year.

[90] 2017 est.

[91] 2016 est.

[92] 2015 est.

Nigeria's agricultural products[93] include cocoa, peanuts, cotton, palm oil, corn, rice, sorghum, millet, cassava (manioc, tapioca), yams, rubber; cattle, sheep, goats, pigs; timber; and fish.

Industries in Nigeria include crude oil, coal, tin, columbite; rubber products, wood; hides and skins, textiles, cement and other construction materials, food products, footwear, chemicals, fertilizer, printing, ceramics, and steel.

As of 2017, industrial production growth rate[94] was estimated at 2.2 percent. Unemployment rate[95] in 2017 was 16.5 percent and in 2016 it was 13.9 percent.

Nigeria's imports-commodities[96] included machinery, chemicals, transport equipment, manufactured goods, food and live animals.

Nigeria's import partners[97] are China 21.1 percent, Belgium 8.7 percent, US 8.4 percent, South Korea 7.5 percent, and UK 4.4 percent.[98]

---

[93] This entry is an ordered listing of major crops and products starting with the most important.

[94] This entry gives the annual percentage increase in industrial production (includes manufacturing, mining, and construction)

[95] This entry contains the percent of the labor force that is without jobs. Substantial underemployment might be noted.

[96] This entry provides a listing of the highest-valued imported products; it sometimes includes the percent of total dollar value.

[97] This entry provides a rank ordering of trading partners starting with the most important; it sometimes includes the percent of total dollar value.

[98] As of 2017, see World fact Book, *supra.*

Its reserves of foreign exchange and gold[99] were US$38.77 billion[100] and US$25.84 billion.[101]

Nigeria's external debt[102] stood at US$40.96 billion[103] and US$31.41 billion.[104]

The average exchange rates[105] of the *Naira* (Nigeria's currency – NGN) *per* US dollar were estimated at 323.5 in 2017, 253 in 2016, 253 in 2015, 192.73 in 2014, and 158.55 in 2013.

---

[99] This entry gives the dollar value for the stock of all financial assets that are available to the central monetary authority for use in meeting a country's balance of payments needs as of the end-date of the period specified. This category includes not only foreign currency and gold, but also a country's holdings of Special Drawing Rights in the International Monetary Fund, and its reserve position in the Fund.

[100] Estimate as of December 31st, 2017.

[101] Estimate as of December 31st, 2016.

[102] This entry gives the total public and private debt owed to non-residents repayable in internationally accepted currencies, goods, or services. These figures are calculated on an exchange rate basis, i.e., not in purchasing power parity (PPP) terms.

[103] As of December 31st, 2017

[104] As of December 31st, 2016

[105] This entry provides the average annual price of a country's monetary unit for the time period specified, expressed in units of local currency per US dollar, as determined by international market forces or by official fiat, and according to the International Organization for Standardization (ISO) 4217 alphabetic currency code. Closing daily exchange rates are not presented in The World Factbook but are used to convert stock values.

Nigeria's energy sources come from electricity, producing some 29.35 billion kWh according to the 2016 estimates, which it neither exports nor imports.[106] It consumes about 24.72 billion kWh.[107] The share of its electricity includes 77 million (2017) population without electricity; 59.3 percent (2016) electrification of the total population; 86 percent (2016) electrification of urban areas; and about 41.1 percent (2016) electrification of rural areas.[108]

Other energy sources include natural gas, crude oil, and refined petroleum products. Carbon dioxide emissions from consumption of energy[109] were estimated at 104 million Mt in 2017.

In terms of communication, Nigeria has 140,491 total fixed telephone lines with a subscriptions per 100 inhabitants of less than 1 per 2018 estimations. However, Nigeria has a total subscription of 172,730,603 for mobile telephones according to 2018 estimates. Generally, the country's telecommunication system can be summarized as follows:

---

[106] See World Fact Book, *supra.*
[107] 2016 est.
[108] World Fact Book, *supra.*
[109] This entry is the total amount of carbon dioxide, measured in metric tons, released by burning fossil fuels in the process of producing and consuming energy.

General assessment: [Nigeria has] one of the larger telecom markets in Africa; most Internet connections are via mobile networks; foreign investment presence, particularly China; market competition; LTE-A technologies available but GSM technology dominate; mobile penetration rate of 123 percent and 173 million subscribers; unified licensing regime; government committed to expanding broadband penetration; in Q1 2018, the Nigerian Communications Commission approved seven licenses to telecom companies to deploy fiber optic cable in the six geopolitical zones and Lagos; operators invest in base stations to take care of network congestion (2020).

Domestic: fixed-line subscribership remains less than 1 per 100 persons; mobile-cellular services growing rapidly, in part responding to the shortcomings of the fixed-line network; multiple cellular providers operate nationally with subscribership base over 85 per 100 persons (2018).

International: country code - 234; landing point for the SAT-3/WASC, NCSCS, MainOne, Glo-1 & 2, ACE, and Equiano fiber-optic submarine cable that provides connectivity to Europe and South and West Africa; satellite earth stations - 3 Intelsat (2 Atlantic Ocean and 1 Indian Ocean) (2019).

The COVID-19 outbreak is negatively impacting telecommunications production and supply chains globally; consumer spending on telecom devices and services has also slowed due to the pandemic's effect on economies worldwide; overall progress towards improvements in all facets of the telecom industry - mobile, fixed-line, broadband, submarine cable and satellite - has moderated.

Broadcast media, nearly 70 federal government-controlled national and regional TV stations; all 36 states operate TV stations; several private TV stations operational; cable and satellite TV subscription services are available; network of federal government-controlled national, regional, and state radio stations; roughly 40 state government-owned radio stations typically carry their own programs except for news broadcasts; about 20 private radio stations; transmissions of international broadcasters are available; digital broadcasting migration process completed in three states in 2018 (2019).[110]

Internet-users account for about 47,759,904 of the population.[111] In terms of roads, Nigeria is said to have the largest road network in West Africa. Nigeria has about 195,000 km of road network of which about 60,000 km are paved.[112]

[110] World Fact Book, *supra.*
[111] *Ibid.*
[112] World Fact Program, "Main domestic and international road corridors. 2.3 Nigeria Road Network. Logistics Capacity Assessments (LCAs)," November 9th, 2017. https://dlca.logcluster.org/display/public/DLCA/2.3+Nigeria+Road+Network

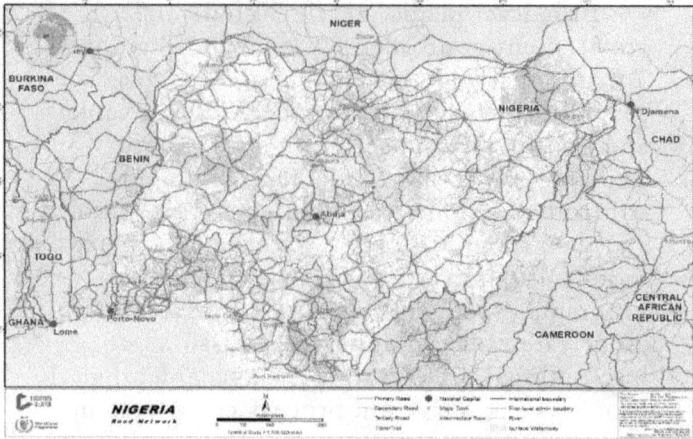

(Source: World Fact Program)

In terms of military, the Nigerian Armed Forces comprises the Army, Navy (includes Coast Guards), Air Force; Ministry of Interior: Nigeria Security and Civil Defence Corps (NSCDC, a paramilitary agency commissioned to assist the military in the management of threats to internal security, including attacks and natural disasters).[113]

Nigeria has approximately 135,000 active personnel (100,000 Army; 20,000 Navy/Coast Guard; 15,000 Air Force); est. 80,000 Security and Civil Defense Corps.[114]

---

[113] As of 2019, see World Fact Book, *supra*.
[114] *Ibid.*

The "Nigerian Armed Forces' inventory consists of a wide variety of imported weapons systems of Chinese, European, Middle Eastern, Russian (including Soviet-era), and US origin; since 2010, the leading suppliers are China, France, Italy, Russia, Ukraine, and the US; Nigeria has been the largest arms importer in sub-Saharan Africa since 2014.

Nigeria is also developing a defense-industry capacity, including small arms, armored personnel vehicle, and small-scale naval production."[115]

As far as military age conscriptions are concerned, 18 years is the age for voluntary military service; Nigeria has no compulsory military conscription.[116] Nigeria has deployed about 200 soldiers to Ghana.

Maritime threat is a problem in Nigeria as summarized by World Fact Book:

---

[115] According to 2019 estimates, *ibid.*
[116] *Ibid.*

The International Maritime Bureau reports the territorial and offshore waters in the Niger Delta and Gulf of Guinea as very high risk for piracy and armed robbery of ships; in 2018, 48 commercial vessels were boarded or attacked compared with 33 attacks in 2017; in 2018, 29 ships were boarded eight of which were underway, 12 were fired upon, and 78 crew members were abducted; Nigerian pirates have extended the range of their attacks to as far away as Cote d'Ivoire and as far as 170 nm offshore; the Maritime Administration of the US Department of Transportation has issued a Maritime Advisory (2019-010-Gulf of Guinea-Piracy/Armed Robbery/Kidnapping for Ransom) effective 19 July 2019, which states in part "Piracy, armed robbery, and kidnapping for ransom (KFR) continue to serve as significant threats to US. flagged vessels transiting or operating in the Gulf of Guinea (GoG).

...According to the Office of Naval Intelligence's "Weekly Piracy Reports" 72 reported incidents of piracy and armed robbery at sea occurred in the GoG region this year as of July 9, 2019. Attacks, kidnappings for ransom (KFR), and boardings to steal valuables from the ships and crews are the most common types of incidents with approximately 75 percent of all incidents taking place off Nigeria. During the first six months of 2019, there were 15 kidnapping and 3 hijackings in the GoG."[117]

---

[117] *Ibid.*

In terms of transportation, Nigeria has about 16 air carriers with about 54 airports.[118] So far as pipelines are concerned, Nigeria has 124 km condensate, 4045 km gas, 164 km liquid petroleum gas, 4441 km oil, 3940 km refined products.[119]

Nigeria has a total of 3,798 km of railways, 195,000 km roadways and 8,600 km waterways. Nigeria's main ports and terminals are at Bonny Inshore Terminal, Calabar, and Lagos.

Terrorism is rampant in Nigeria:

> Boko Haram: aim(s): [to] replace the Nigerian Government with an Islamic state under strict sharia and, ultimately, establish an Islamic caliphate across Africa; avenge military offenses against the group and destroy any political or social activity associated with Western society; conducts attacks against primarily civilian and regional military targets area(s) of operation: headquartered in the northeast. [Since] 2009, fighters have killed tens of thousands of Nigerians during hundreds of attacks and disrupted trade and farming in the northeast, causing a risk of famine and displacing millions of people; violently opposes any political or social activity associated with Western society, including voting, attending secular schools, and wearing Western dress....Islamic State of Iraq and ash-Sham (ISIS)-West Africa: aim(s):

---

[118] Claimants must know the exact airport from which they boarded their plane to come to Canada.

[119] According to 2019 estimates, *supra*.

implement ISIS's strict interpretation of
Sharia; replace the Nigerian Government with
an Islamic state...area(s) of operation: based
primarily in the north along the border with
Niger, with its largest presence in the
northeast and the Lake Chad region; targets
primarily regional military installations and
civilians.[120]

International disputes and local refugee issues are rife:

Joint Border Commission with Cameroon
reviewed 2002 ICJ ruling on the entire
boundary and bilaterally resolved differences,
including June 2006 Greentree Agreement that
immediately cedes sovereignty of the Bakassi
Peninsula to Cameroon with a phaseout of
Nigerian control within two years while
resolving patriation issues; the ICJ ruled on an
equidistance settlement of Cameroon-
Equatorial Guinea-Nigeria maritime boundary
in the Gulf of Guinea, but imprecisely defined
coordinates in the ICJ decision and a
sovereignty dispute between Equatorial
Guinea and Cameroon over an island at the
mouth of the Ntem River all contribute to the
delay in implementation; only Nigeria and
Cameroon have heeded the Lake Chad
Commission's admonition to ratify the
delimitation treaty which also includes the
Chad-Niger and Niger-Nigeria boundaries;
location of Benin-Niger-Nigeria tripoint is
unresolved.[121]

---

[120] *Ibid.*
[121] *Ibid.*

Nigeria has about 44,524 refugees, mostly from Cameroon, as of 2019. Nigeria has about 3,214,506 internally displaced persons (IDPs). Most of these are from "northeast Nigeria; Boko Haram attacks and counterinsurgency efforts in northern Nigeria; communal violence between Christians and Muslims in the middle belt region, political violence; flooding; forced evictions; cattle rustling; competition for resources."[122]

In terms of illicit drugs, Nigeria is a "a transit point for heroin and cocaine intended for European, East Asian, and North American markets; consumer of amphetamines; safe haven for Nigerian narcotraffickers operating worldwide; major money-laundering center; massive corruption and criminal activity; Nigeria has improved some anti-money-laundering controls, resulting in its removal from the Financial Action Task Force's (FATF's) Noncooperative Countries and Territories List in June 2006; Nigeria's anti-money-laundering regime continues to be monitored by FATF."[123]

---

[122] According to 2020 report, *ibid.*
[123] *Ibid.*

5| IFA AND THE LAW

> IFA is always an issue if a claim
> originated from Nigeria. There is only
> one exception, if the claimant became
> aware of persecution while already out of
> Nigeria.

Revocation of Jurisprudential Guide

IFA may be analyzed differently depending on the nature of persecution and the political construction of the country vis-à-vis the type of agents of persecution. This is especially notable for persons fleeing persecution from non-state actors. Nigeria is one of the countries where IFA is a relevant issue in most refugee claim cases.

In April 2020, IRB revoked the identification of Decision TB7-19851 as a Jurisprudential Guide (JG). IRB found that, "Developments in the country of origin information related to the Nigeria JG [had] diminished the value of the decision as a JG."[124]

In Nigeria, RPD required that a Claimant who feared persecution in one part of the country, say in Abuja, should exhaust all other cities where they could be free from persecution within Nigeria, say Port Harcourt, before seeking for refugee protection in Canada. That was the *ratio* in TB7-19851 rendered by RPD Member, Gamble, on May 17th, 2018.

The decision found that, based on the documentary evidence available at the time, there were several large cities in Nigeria that might, depending on the facts of the case, serve as viable IFAs for persons fleeing non-state actors.

The IRB determined that, TB7-19851 is no longer binding but is still persuasive. In other words, it is identified as a RAD Reasons of Interest (RROI).

TB7-19851 will, therefore, be used as persuasive decision for determining the issue of IFA in Nigeria. Nigeria, unlike Iran where IFA is not available owing to the fact that the same State apparatus controls the entire country, is a federation of different States. As such, there might be an IFA, "...in major cities in south and central Nigeria for claimants fleeing non-state actors."[125]

---

[124] IRB, "Notice of Revocation of a Jurisprudential Guide," < https://irb-cisr.gc.ca/en/news/2020/Pages/notice-revocation-jurisprudential-guide.aspx> (accessed on April 30th, 2020)
[125] *Ibid.*

IRB further determined that, "Developments in the country of origin information, including those in relation to the ability of *single women* to relocate to the various internal flight alternatives proposed in the Nigeria jurisprudential guide, [had] diminished the value of the decision as a jurisprudential guide"[126] Accordingly, as of April 6th, 2020, the identification of TB7-19851 as a JG was revoked. The decision, though, remains a persuasive RROI for future determinations.

An important note to the reader, this revocation does not preclude the RPD and the RAD from considering IFA in refugee claims for Nigerians. If raised at the hearing, either through intensive questioning or counsel's submissions, the claimant is still required to fully answer and defend their claims with regards to IFA.

IFA Persuasive in Nigeria

IFA for Nigerian claimants is still persuasive and the adjudicator may consider the availability of IFA in the context of the case presented. Counsel and the claimant should prepare for this aspect of the refugee determination and be ready to provide answer if asked.

---

[126] *Ibid.* (emphasis added).

The question of whether an IFA exists is an integral part of the Convention refugee definition. The key concepts concerning IFA come from two cases: *Rasaratnam*[127] and *Thirunavukkarasu*.[128]

From these cases it is clear that the test to be applied in determining whether there is an IFA is two-pronged: "… the Board must be satisfied on a balance of probabilities that there is no serious possibility of the appellant being persecuted in the part of the country to which it finds an IFA exists."

Moreover, conditions in the part of the country considered to be an IFA must be such that it would not be unreasonable, in all the circumstances, including those particular to the appellant, for her to seek refuge there.

Two-prongs IFA Test

First leg:

---

[127] *Rasaratnam v Canada* (Minister of Employment and Immigration) (CA), [1992] 1 FC 706, [1991] FCJ No 1256; see also case summary in the Cases Cited section.
[128] *Thirunavukkarasu v Canada* (Minister of Employment and Immigration) (CA), [1994] 1 FC 589, [1993] FCJ No 1172, 1993 CanLII 3011; see also case summary in the Cases Cited section.

"... the Board must be satisfied on a balance of probabilities that there is no serious possibility of the claimant being persecuted in the part of the country to which it finds an IFA exists."[129]

Second leg:

"...conditions in the part of the country considered to be an IFA must be such that it would not be unreasonable, in all the circumstances, including those particular to the claimant, for him to seek refuge there."[130]

Case Study

The case requires the examination of whether Principal Appellant (PA) and Associate Appellant (AA) had no IFA in Lagos and Port Harcourt, two metropolitan cities in Nigeria.

---

[129] *Rasaratnam, supra*, note 1 at 710. In *Chowdhury, Swapan v. M.C.I.* (F.C., no. IMM-5618-06), de Montigny, January 8, 2008; 2008 FC 18, the Court noted that it is an error to require a claimant to show that persecution in the IFA "would" happen. See also *Sokol, Sterbyci v. M.C.I.* (F.C., no. IMM-1767-09), O'Keefe, December 8, 2009; 2009 FC 1257. In *Iqbal, Sherry v. M.C.I.* (F.C., no. IMM-3224-17), McDonald, March 15, 2018; 2018 FC 299 the Court quashed a visa officer's decision because his statement that there was a "low risk" that the applicant would be harmed in the IFA location did not allow the Court to determine that he had applied the correct test.
[130] *Ibid.*, at 709 and 711

The Court of Appeal in *Kanagaratnam* was of the view that the determination of whether an Appellant has a well-founded fear of persecution in her home area of the country is not a prerequisite to the consideration of an IFA.

At the same time, if an Appellant fails to meet elements of the definition in the home area, it is open to the Board not to proceed to do an IFA analysis. In other words, if the Appellant fails to establish a subjective fear, it is not necessary to make an IFA analysis. An Appellant must first *establish a subjective fear for an IFA analysis to be performed.*

The concept of an IFA does not require that the haven is in another city or province of the state of origin so long as it is truly an area in which the Appellant can seek refuge from the experienced persecution.

In other words, an IFA can still exist in the same country, province, or town in which the Appellant has experienced persecution. Therefore, the Appellant must satisfy the Member that there is no IFA in their country, province, or town even before the Appellant looks to other countries for safety. At the same time, an IFA may still exist where the risks in the proposed IFA are risks faced by all inhabitants.

In short, the risks must not be of general nature but specific to the Appellant's case. If everyone is exposed and suffers from similar dangers in that area, an IFA analysis will fail.

It is submitted in this case at bar that the Appellant had no IFA either in their State (Lagos) or Port Harcourt, though the AA had due diligently relocated to two towns in Lagos State. New evidence satisfies the non-existence of IFA in Port Harcourt for the Appellants.

There is a live arrest warrant for PA, AA's aunt was attacked in Port Harcourt by PA's uncle, and PA's uncle has business investments in Port Harcourt.

A finding of IFA must be based on a distinct evaluation of a region for that purpose taking into account the Appellant's identity. It cannot be inferred from earlier findings of fact unconnected to the issue of an IFA. The relationship between IFA, change of circumstances, and the applicability of "compelling reasons" was considered by the Court, which concluded that where an IFA applies to an Appellant, that person is not and never could have been a Convention refugee. Accordingly, he or she could not cease to be a Convention refugee on the basis of a change of circumstances.

If an Appellant had an IFA, they could not become a refugee. And if that Appellant became a refugee because he had no IFA and then at some point after the claim is successful and an IFA becomes available in their home country, that refugee Appellant cannot have their refugee status revoked. It is submitted based on one new evidence proffered herein, that the Appellant had no IFA when she came to Canada and still does not have one in Nigeria currently and in the future.

PA had already been in the US when his uncle decided to abduct his children and beat up his wife. He knew while in the US that his life was in danger in Nigeria and, therefore, decided, rather, to make it possible for his family to join him in the US.

Concerning notice, the issue of IFA must be raised by the Member or the Minister (before or during the hearing). The Act does not automatically put Appellants on notice that IFA is an issue in the claim.

The principles regarding fair notice of giving proper notice, as expressed in *Rasaratnam* and *Thirunavukkarasu* are still relevant under the Act.

The notice must be clear and sufficient. It is submitted here that the Member did not violate this precept. However, the Appellant submits that no viable IFA is available for the Appellants in Port Harcourt as proven by new evidence.

With respect to the burden of proof, once the issue is raised, the onus is on the Appellant to show that she does not have an IFA. Even though the burden of proof rests on the Appellant, the Board cannot base a finding that there is an IFA, in the absence of sufficient evidence, solely on the basis that the Appellant has not fulfilled the onus of proof.

There is no onus on an Appellant to personally test the viability of an IFA before seeking protection in Canada.

While in earlier jurisprudence there was inconsistency about whether a specific location or region must be identified as the potential IFA, more recent case law suggests that the RPD *must* identify the specific IFA locations.

The outcome of any one particular judicial review application involving this issue may hinge on how clearly the Appellant was questioned regarding the IFA issue and how clearly the Member explains its findings.

It is submitted that, in this case, the Appellant discharged the burden. However, PA did not need to personally go back to Port Harcourt from the US just to test the IFA.

Similarly, AA and the children had relocated to two cities before they joined PA in the US. There was no need for AA and the children to go and test IFA in Port Harcourt before they joined PA in the US.

It is further submitted that the Member did not error in choosing Port Harcourt as a possible viable IFA. However, the Member errored in requiring that the Appellants test IFA in Port Harcourt before coming to Canada

The abundance of case law on the topic of IFA concerns the interpretation and application of the two-pronged test. Some factors are relevant to both prongs of the test, some are relevant to one or the other prong.

On the issue of whether there is a serious possibility of persecution in the potential IFA, the considerations are basically the same as when making this determination concerning the Appellant's home area of the country. However, there are some specific points concerning this issue and IFA that are noteworthy.

In determining whether there is an objective basis for fearing persecution in the IFA, the Board must consider the personal circumstances of the Appellants, and not just general evidence concerning other persons who live there.

It is submitted that in this case, the Member failed to apply the "personal circumstances of the Appellant" to this case. AA had already been beaten, raped, and made to miscarry. In addition, she had two young children. Her husband was in the US. She ran away to two towns before joining her husband in the US.

The nature and the agents of the persecution feared ought to suggest that the persecution would be confined to particular areas of the country.

If an individual had to remain in hiding to avoid problems, this would not be evidence of an IFA. On the contrary, the Appellants ran to different places in search of safety but were found by the agents of persecution.

The presence of close relatives in the putative IFA, and the duration of the previous residence and past employment there, may have a bearing on "whether or not it is 'objectively reasonable' for the Appellant to live in … [the IFA] without fear of persecution," rather than being matters merely of personal comfort or convenience.

In this case, AA had minor children and sought IFA among a friend of the husband and relative, but when it was more dangerous, she joined the husband who was already safe in the US.

Large urban areas cannot be assumed to be an IFA by virtue of their population size alone. In this case, the Member errored by simply considering Port Harcourt an urban center and assume that it would be a more viable IFA for the Appellants than other areas she relocated to. New evidence shows that the Appellants would be arrested or harmed in Port Harcourt. PA's uncle has substantial investments there, his famous daughter lives there, he recently visited there, and AA's aunt was beaten up there and she is presently in hiding.

Reasonable in All the Circumstances

The second prong of the IFA test may be stated as follows: *Would it be unduly harsh to expect the appellant to move to another, less hostile part of the country before seeking refugee status abroad?*

The test is an objective one: Is it objectively reasonable to expect the Appellant to seek safety in a different part of the country? *Thirunavukkarasu* sets a very high threshold for what makes an IFA unreasonable in all the circumstances.

The hardship associated with dislocation and relocation is not the kind of undue hardship that renders an IFA unreasonable.

The standard is high and requires proof of adverse conditions that would jeopardize the life and safety of the Appellant in traveling to and in living in the IFA location.

It is submitted herein that in this case, and argued, it would be objectively difficult to relocate to Port Harcourt where the cost of living and accommodation is very high (two years rent payment is required in advance) and the Appellants faced persecution. Cost of living in Port Harcourt is described as "very high... very expensive... astronomical cost of housing...."[131]

An IFA cannot be speculative or theoretical only; it must be a realistic, attainable option. The Appellant cannot be required to encounter great physical danger or to undergo undue hardship in traveling there or staying there. However, it is not enough for the Appellant to say that he or she does not like the weather there, or that he or she has no friends or relatives there, or that he or she may not be able to find suitable work there. It is submitted that the key reason why Port Harcourt would not be a viable IFA is that the Appellants would be harmed here, just as AA's aunt was beaten up for refusing to disclose the whereabouts of AA.

---

[131] See Exhibit "22" under "Cost of Living," "Employment," and "Housing."

A distinction must be maintained between the reasonableness of an IFA and humanitarian and compassionate considerations. The fact that an Appellant might be better off in Canada, physically, economically, and emotionally than in a safe place in her own country is not a factor to consider in assessing the reasonableness of the IFA.

Indeed, as testified, the only reason the Appellant could not find an IFA in Port Harcourt is safety. The sole reason for coming to Canada was to seek safety from persecution. In fact, the psychological outlook of these Appellants only worsens because of the "traumatic experience they both endured while in Nigeria," and AA is a victim of rape in Nigeria and both are "being traumatized, [have] a feeling of depressed mood and anxiety."[132]

Regarding the issue of "reasonable in all the circumstances," the Court of Appeal has stated that the circumstances must be relevant to the IFA question. They cannot be cataloged in the abstract. They will vary from case to case. The Federal Court has provided the following general guidance.

The test is a flexible one that takes into account the particular situation of the Appellant and the particular country involved. The evidence, before the Refugee Division, of circumstances in the IFA must be more than general information and must be relevant to the Appellant's specific circumstances. The Appellants submits that they met and meet this test.

---

[132] See Exhibit "17", psychological report dated August 31st, 2020, esp. pages 3 and 4

The Appellants surmise that, unlike in *Rasaratnam, supra.*, where Rasaratnam had lived in Colombo safely for six months in 1989 and had failed to discharge his burden of proof, in this case, however, PA left Nigeria for the US before the threats intensified and did not need to return to Nigeria. AA, on the other hand, had run to two other places before she was located by her persecutors. She joined PA in the US. It is submitted that the Appellants have successfully discharged the burden of proof in this case.

The Appellants further submit that this case at bar is similar in principle to *Thirunavukkarasu, supra*. There, the Court approved the appeal and concluded that the evidence presented showed enough indication that the Appellant, Mr. Thirunavukkarasu, had a well-founded fear of persecution on the basis of political opinion in North of Sri Lanka.

Additionally, he had also proven on a balance of probabilities that he would face the serious risk of persecution in Colombo from the Sri Lankan government based on race. Thereby, declaring him to be a Convention refugee. This case may be similar to *Rasaratnam*, but the judge reiterated that the determination of the case was reached by solely relying on the evidence presented before the Court, and regarding the circumstances faced by this particular Appellant.

In *Singh, supra.*, Mr. Gurmeet Singh had experienced several incidents of harassment, vandalism, arrests, and detention against him because of his involvement with a religious group. Moreover, his psychological report, the Court decided, *should have been taken into consideration.* These Appellants submit that their case is similar in principle to *Singh* and must be accepted.

The Appellants submit, and the fact is, that the Member failed to consider the psychological report with fairness. The Court has ruled that psychological evidence is central to the question of whether an IFA is reasonable and cannot be disregarded.[133] The Member had completely disregarded this report.

---

[133] *Cartagena, Wilber Orlando v. M.C.I.* (F.C., no. IMM-961-06), Mosley, March 4, 2008; 2008 FC 289 [Case not provided; Appellant invokes RAD takes judicial notice of this case]

6 | VIOLENCE AND HEALTH CARE

There are many issues that may fall under the Convention refugee ground of "membership in a particular social group," including violence, healthcare, FGM and chieftaincy. This chapter will only provide a cursory view of violence and healthcare. FGM and chieftaincy will be dealt with in the second edition.

Boko Haram and Stolen Medical Supplies

On Christmas Eve 2020, **Boko Haram** militants killed several people in Borno State in north-eastern Nigeria. During raids on mostly Christian villages, the militants stole medical supplies from a hospital in Pemi before setting it on fire.

They also burned down a church and abducted a priest. The Safeguarding Health in Conflict Coalition (SHCC) identified 43 incidents of violence against or obstruction of health care in Nigeria in 2020, compared to 19 such incidents in 2019. Health workers were kidnapped, and health supplies looted.

Some doctors and nurses have reportedly left their clinical positions and others have gone on strike in response to the targeted kidnapping of physicians. The loss of these health workers has had a profound effect on the country's health services. The presence of **Boko Haram** in *Adamawa, Borno,* and *Yobe* states continued to affect health workers and health centers in 2020. Boko Haram uses an Islamist ideology to oppose the Nigerian governments and other states. Violent tactics, including looting and kidnapping for ransom, sustain the group's operations, are used.

Boko Haram also operates in Cameroon, Chad, and Niger. The growing presence of **armed groups** – locally referred to as "bandits" – in Katsina, Kaduna, and Zamfara states adversely affects healthcare and health workers.

These "bandits" are believed to have set up camps in Rugu forest in Zamfara state, which they use as a springboard for attacks on rural communities to steal cattle and food supplies or to carry out ambushes on roads. They often kill those who resist kidnapping.

There are some concerns that these groups, which operate mainly for financial profit, may have been infiltrated by extremists. Communal conflicts between **herder and farmer** communities, as well as ethno-religious conflicts, also affect health workers. Health workers were kidnapped in southern Nigeria, where kidnappings for profit are common. Nigerian Armed

Forces personnel also injured a health worker.[134]

HIV/AIDS

In 2020, there were 1.7 million people with HIV; 1.3 percent adult HIV prevalence; 86,000 new HIV infections; 49,000 AIDS-related deaths; and 1.5 million people on antiretroviral treatment.[135]

Nigeria introduced a range of support to help people stay on HIV treatment, including Peer Treatment Champions and Mentor Mothers – and these measures are working. In just one year (2019 to 2020) the number of people with HIV who were virally suppressed jumped by around 10 percent.[136]

In 2015, Nigeria began addressing gender inequality through its national HIV prevention strategy. Reducing violence and coercion and increasing legal protection for women and girls are focus areas.[137]

Since 2019, Nigeria has been providing free HIV self-testing kits for population groups most at risk of HIV and the male partners of women with HIV.

---

[134] https://reliefweb.int/sites/reliefweb.int/files/resources/2021-SHCC-Nigeria.pdf
[135] https://www.beintheknow.org/understanding-hiv-epidemic/data/glance-hiv-nigeria
[136] *Ibid.*
[137] *Ibid.*

In 2020, it extended its self-testing program to include adolescents and young people.[138] Late diagnosis of HIV is a problem in Nigeria: around one-third of people are only diagnosed when HIV has progressed to AIDS. So, in 2019 Nigeria began offering specialized support for people who start antiretroviral treatment with a low CD4 count.[139]

As argued in Chapter 2, HIV-AIDS and related healthcare issues may constitute either discrimination or persecution depending on the situation of each particular case. Counsel representing claimants on these issues must analyze the story and evidence available to determine whether a claimant has made a case for refugee claim.

Property Grabbing and Gender-Related Issues

Women are still routinely being cut out of their parents' inheritance in parts of south-eastern Nigeria, despite a Supreme Court ruling that it is discriminatory. The Nigerian constitution prohibits such gender-based discrimination but many Igbo people still stick to their traditions.

In most families, property left behind by fathers is divided among male children - the size of each

---

[138] Ibid.
[139] Ibid.

person's share is determined by age so older siblings tend to get more - and women are excluded.

In some cases where shares are given to women, they are limited to things owned by their mothers and cannot inherit lands and houses.[140]

The IRB has created the "Chairperson's Guideline 4: Gender Considerations in Proceedings Before the Immigration and Refugee Board,"[141] (hereafter the "Guideline") to minimize stereotypes labeled against to women who may be caught up in abusive and "myths, stereotypes, and incorrect assumptions in decision-making, particularly when making credibility findings."[142]

Historically, women who brought claims for refugee protection in Canada suffered from these incorrect interpretations of myths and stereotypes because of their gender.

The Guideline applies to:

> ...women refugee claimants. This Guideline broadens the focus to include all genders and gender identities, while recognizing that women and girls and SOGIESC (sexual orientation, gender identity and expression and sex characteristics) individuals are disproportionately impacted by gender-based violence, gender inequality and discrimination, all of which are human rights issues.[143]

---

[140] https://www.bbc.com/news/world-africa-55675987
[141] https://irb.gc.ca/en/legal-policy/policies/Pages/GuideDir04.aspx?=undefined&wbdisable=false#s1 accessed on October 9th, 2023.
[142] *Ibid.*
[143] *Ibid.*

Not only does the Guideline debunk myths and stereotypes, but it also defines traumas and provides principled trauma-informed adjudication, procedural accommodations, and takes a participatory and intersectional approach to the finding of credibility in refugee hearings concerning the identified affected groups.

In terms of corroboration evidence, the Guideline provides the following assistance to adjudicators:

> ...Members should be alert to the difficulties faced by survivors of gender-based violence when considering whether corroborative evidence could be reasonably expected to be available. In cases of gender-based violence, individuals may face difficulty obtaining corroborative evidence in the form of personal disclosure for several reasons including shame, stigma, secrecy, and the cycle of power and control that can often contribute to such violence. In some cases, due to the deeply personal nature of the abuse, and the potential trauma associated with it, the only evidence available may be the individual's own testimony.[144]

Foreign documents are addressed in the Guideline in this way:

> ...Foreign documents should be considered based on their contents, and the level of detail that can be expected is highly contextual. For example, brevity in a police report regarding an

---

[144] *Ibid.*

accusation of sexual violence should not
automatically be assumed to indicate lack of
credibility. Instead, the brevity may indicate
lack of police interest in the complaint.[145]

Drawing of a negative inference from an officer's notes, the assessment of the specific contents of the expert reports (such as medical, psychological or social) and the member's reasons for the decision should be explained in the decision. The Guideline also provides for the separation of the hearing with co-parties who might potentially be affected due to stigma, physical harm, or ostracization by family members.

The Guideline provides the following advisory on state protection:

> The claimant's subjective reluctance to seek
> state protection does not necessarily rebut the
> presumption of state protection. Individuals
> who experience gender-based violence may not
> seek assistance or state protection, due to past
> negative experiences with state authorities,
> internalized and community shame, fear of not
> being believed, or personal risks associated with
> seeking assistance. Lack of freedom of
> movement and discriminatory laws and policies
> may also constitute barriers to seeking state
> protection.[146]

This is dubbed a *contextual and intersectional approach* to the determination of credibility in cases involving women and girls.

---

[145] *Ibid.*
[146] *Ibid.*

On IFA, the Guideline provides:

> The safety of an IFA is dependent on the claimant's personal profile. For example, a claimant may face a greater risk as a single woman, divorced woman, widow, or single parent. Members should also consider the cycle of violence and coercive control when assessing whether an agent of harm may have the motivation and means to locate a claimant.[147]

An intersectional approach in determining credibility is advised.[148]

As argued in Chapter 2, HIV-AIDS and related healthcare issues may constitute either discrimination or persecution depending on the situation of each particular case. Counsel representing claimants on these issues must analyze the story and evidence available to determine whether a claimant has made a refugee claim.

[147] *Ibid.*
[148] *Ibid.*

7 | HOMOSEXUALITY IN NIGERIA

> This chapter is not exhaustive on sexual-orientation issues. Homosexuality in Nigeria affects gays, lesbians and bisexuals.

Homosexuality Considered Demonic

" Any sexual orientation that is not heterosexual is considered unnatural, demonic, and immoral" in Nigeria and that there are "laws, policies, and cultures that police people's sexuality."[149] Such a law was the 2013 *Same-Sex Marriage (Prohibition) Act.* This law, clearly, proscribes homosexuality in Nigeria. Conviction for a same-sex activity is punishable by up to 14 years in prison.

Case Study

---

[149] NGA105219.E, 6.7

A male claimant, Mr. Ondejagbo, was involved in a homosexual relationship in Nigeria. Mr. Ondejagbo was a married man and he had two children with his wife. His wife did not know that Mr. Ondejagbo was bisexual until a personal disaster happened to Mr. Ondejagbo.

The Nigerian government and society consider homosexuality as "unnatural, sinful and an abomination."

Although bisexuality is rarely named as such in Nigeria, there are people whose lives and self-conceptions could fairly be described as "bisexual."

The male claimant here is such a one. And he is not perceived any more favorably than homosexuality in Nigeria. There is no middle ground, a person must be either homosexual or heterosexual.

In the context of marriage, homosexuals are under pressure to marry: "[M]arriage in the cultural context of Nigeria is not negotiable. There is immense social and familial pressure from parents, siblings, grandparents, religious communities to marry, often to secure a bride price."

Therefore, both Mr. Ondejagbo and the late Tefiola had to marry and maintain their affairs in secret. Like Mr. Ondejagbo and Tefiola, "LGBT people have been marrying members of the opposite sex to avoid accusations of being homosexual."

In terms of societal treatment, "there were reports of increased threats and harassment against LGBT people." "The majority of people who are bisexual are not open or remain hidden, LGBT people hide their orientation 'deeply' for fear of discrimination."

Thus, "bisexuals who are discovered to be engaging in same-sex activity face the same risks of mistreatment that gays and lesbians in Nigeria encounter."

And as testified, Mr. Ondejagbo was beaten up, and his partner, sadly, was killed. And this falls in tandem with the objective information gathered for Nigeria, namely, that, "bisexuals who are discovered to be engaging in same same-sex activity risk being 'lynched, beaten, arrested, ostracized, and disowned by family and community.'"

The authorities, similarly, ill-treat people perceived to be LGBT. Thus, "'both the police and the Islamic police (HISPA) are seen as eager to arrest homosexuals' and although they reportedly do not 'actively' try to identify them, suspects arrested for homosexuality are 'put under considerable pressure to confess' by police."

Had Mr. Ondejagbo been arrested, he would have been under pressure, "and the chances of getting a fair trial once arrested or prosecuted [for same-sex acts] would have been non-existent."

The same NDP seem to suggest that wives or husbands of bisexuals, if they discover that their partner was bisexual, may divorce their bisexual partner. In this case, however, none of the partners to Mr. Ondejagbo or Mr. Tefiola discovered or knew that their husbands were bisexual.

It, therefore, and partly, explains why Mrs. Ondejagbo is in serious danger in Nigeria – because she is perceived as having known her husband was bisexual and did not report him or divorce him.

The NDP sates, "Sources state that if someone is bisexual and married, they risk losing their partner, spouse and children." If he had remained in Nigeria, Mr. Ondejagbo would have faced "family rejection" as well.

Similarly, the NDP states that, "reports of 'attacks aimed at expelling persons from villages and neighborhoods.'" This also explains why Mr. Ondejagbo would have faced "mob violence" in Aguata, a village where he had escaped to in order to hide. At this village, as testified and stated in the BOC narrative, "A man among the group who looked like a resident of my area in Anambra East…shouted, 'Is this not the man that is being searched for in Anambra East…'" Indeed, Mr. Ondejagbo was in trouble in this village, just as he would have been anywhere in Nigeria.

And as testified, when he arrived in Aguata, between 1 am and 3 am, he was questioned by the vigilantes. According to NDP, "There are no legal constraints on movement within the country, however government-imposed curfews and insecurity in areas" are common in some parts of Nigeria. And "Freedoms of internal movement and foreign travel are legally guaranteed. However, security officials frequently impose dusk-to-dawn curfews and other movement restrictions in areas affected by communal violence."[150]

---

[150] CPN, 5.1.5

Further, the NDP is categorical on healthcare provision to bisexuals: "LGBT people face discrimination from healthcare providers and may be denied care or encounter insensitivity to their health needs." *Discrimination* is not the factor here, but the *persecution* that ensues because of it.

This is the reason why Mr. Ondejagbo did not disclose the source of his injuries when he attended at Askira Medical Center for the treatment of his wounds.

Indeed, "It is not a standard practice in Nigeria for a Commissioner of Oaths to swear an affidavit regarding a person's gender or sexual orientation."[151]

And there is nowhere mentioned or even testified that the friend of Mr. Ondejagbo's (Okonkwo Assane) had sworn an affidavit or commissioned an oath regarding the bisexuality of the claimant.

"'It would be strange' for a person to swear to an affidavit about sexual orientation because these are crimes in Nigeria and would 'amount to ... reporting himself or herself to the law.'"

Ms. Assane never did that.

There is no such evidence at this hearing that an affidavit to that effect existed.

---

[151] 6.10

There is proof that Ms. Assane is a lawyer in Nigeria and is consequently a member of the Lagos NBA. However, in this claim, she is only relevant to the fact that she assisted with travel agency matters as well as unofficially alerting the claimant to the dangers he would face if he remained in Nigeria, vis-à-vis, the law and perception of bisexuals in Nigeria.

Similarly, when the widow of Tefiola was contacted to confirm if she had known Mr. Ondejagbo since 2003, she did not swear an affidavit but only wrote a letter after much persuasion to do so. This is because, according to 6.10, "families of an LGBT person 'first want to save themselves the embarrassment and stigma associated with homosexuality' and would thus avoid obtaining or swearing to such an affidavit."

Refugee Surplace: Claims may also be advanced based, in whole or part, on the activities of the claimant since leaving his or her country. *Urur, Mohamed Ahmed v. M.E.I*[152] and *Cai, Heng Ye v. M.C.I.*,[153] are on point in this case.

The Court underscored the importance of considering the claimant's activities both in the home country and abroad in combination. I submit that Mr. Ondejagbo is credible, and also has advanced an alternative, that you should consider his continuous activities in the LGTB continuity in Canada pursuant to *Barry, Abdoulaye v. M.C.I.*[154]

---

[152] (F.C.A., no. A-228-87), January 15th, 1988
[153] (F.C.T.D., no. IMM-1088-96), May 16th, 1997
[154] (F.C.T.D., no. IMM-573-01), Pinard, February 26th, 2002.

Overall, and on the issue central to this hearing, namely, credibility, Mr. Ondejagbo testified in a straightforward manner, coherently and cogently. He adduced clear and unambiguous evidence. His testimony was consistent with the NDP objective evidence on Nigeria.

Moreover, there were no material inconsistencies – there was one or two places where Mr. Ondejagbo could have made mention of an individual or given more information, even in those cases, Mr. Ondejagbo was able to provide reasonable explanation. There was no attempt at misleading the Panel or embellishing the evidence.

Mr. Ondejagbo has provided clear and convincing evidence; that he is a person who belongs to a particular social group, namely, bisexuality. He is afraid of returning to Nigeria for the fear of being arrested or accosted. In addition, he has continued to find assistance on his orientation in Canada via 519 and similar-situated LGTB organizations; and that, on the balance of probabilities, he is both a Convention refugee pursuant to section 96 of the Act,[155] and a person in need of protection pursuant to subsection 97(1) of the Act.[156]

With those submissions, I respectfully implore the Panel to accept Mr. Ondejagbo as a Convention refugee and a person in need of protection in Canada.

---

[155] *Immigration and Refugee Protection Act, supra.*
[156] *Ibid.*

8 | CREDIBLE NIGERIAN DOCUMENTS

> Refugee claimants who are providing documents to the RPD must be aware that the RPD has access to sample Nigerian documents. The meticulousness and thoroughness required to prepare and provide these documents is part of the credibility establishing process at the RPD. Small details matter, and both counsels and claimants must ensure that they countercheck and inspect documents originating from Nigeria to preserve the dignity and worth of the Canadian refugee determination system.

Obtaining a SIM Card

The Nigerian Communications Commission Regulations,[157] 2011, provides that mobile telephone service providers must capture and register the "biometrics and other personal

---

[157] Also known as Registration of Telephone Subscribers Regulations

information" of their customers before activating a new SIM card.[158]

The data is then uploaded to a central database administered by the National Communication Commission (NCC).[159] According to sources, facial image and fingerprints are required as biometric information that must be provided for [telephone] subscribers.[160]

Opening a Bank Account

According to their respective websites, Nigerian banks Zenith Bank and Guaranty Trust Bank (GTBank) request the following to open a bank account:

- One [recent] passport photo
- Identification document: driver's license, passport or national ID card [or Voter's Card[161] or "any other acceptable identification document deemed fit by the bank"[162]
- Two references
- Utility bill issued within the last three months (Zenith Bank and GTBank)

---

[158] Nigeria 2011, Art. 11-12
[159] Nigeria 2011, Art. 6
[160] https://irb-cisr.gc.ca/en/country-information/rir/Pages/index.aspx?doc=457725
[161] Zenith Bank n.d.a
[162] GTBank n.d.a

The same banks indicate on their respective "[a]ccount [o]pening" forms that the customer applying for a bank account must provide the following information:

- Branch and account number
- Bank Verification Number (BVN)
- Personal information: title, surname, first name, other names, mother's maiden name, date and place of birth, gender, nationality, state of origin, marital status, local government area (LGA) [of origin (GTBank)], Tax ID number (TIN), phone number(s), email address, residential address (including state, LGA and city/town), residence permit number, residence permit issue and expiry dates, means of identification [(National ID card, driver's license, passport, Voter's Card or other) and number of the ID document (Zenith Bank)], ID document issue and expiry dates.
- Details of next of kin: title, names and surname, date of birth, gender, relationship, phone numbers, email address and home address.
- Employment details: employment status, annual salary/expected annual income, employer's name and address.
- Additional details: name(s) of "[b]eneficial [o]wner(s) (if any)," sources of funds to the

account [and "[o]ther [s]ources of [i]ncome (if any)" (Zenith Bank)] (Zenith Bank; GTBank).

In addition to the GTBank's form requests, the following information is required:

- Personal information: educational level, name and birth date of first child, whether the customer has citizenship or residency in any other country, and social security number; Additional details: spouse's name if applicable, spouse's date of birth, spouse's occupation, [spouse's] phone numbers, sources of funds to the account, name of associated business(es) (if any), type of business and business address.
- Information on accounts held with other banks.

Zenith Bank's form also lists the following fields of information:

- Home town; "[r]eligion (optional)" (Zenith).[163]

Bank Verification Number (BVN)

According to sources, the BVN project aims to create a unique identity number for each person

---

[163] *Ibid.*

holding bank account(s) in Nigeria.[164] For more information on the BVN, see Response to Information Request.[165]

Telecommunications in Nigeria

Nigeria 2023 population is estimated at 223,804,632 people at midyear. Nigeria population is equivalent to 2.78 percent of the total world population. Nigeria ranks number six in the list of countries (and dependencies) by population.[166]

The Bertelsmann Stiftung's Transformation Index (BTI) 2020, which "assesses the transformation toward democracy and market economy as well as the quality of governance in 137 countries," indicated that at the end of 2018, "active mobile phone subscriptions exceeded 150 million."[167]

A 2018 report on Nigeria's digital economy by the Global System for Mobile Communications (GSM) Association (GSMA), an organization that "represents the interests of mobile operators worldwide,"[168] indicated that as of September 2018 there were 97.5 million unique mobile subscribers, 53 million

---

[164] Paradigm Initiative and Privacy International Mar. 2018, para. 36; NIBSS n.d.
[165] NGA106108 of May 2018.
[166] Worldometer, "Nigeria Population 2023."
[167] Bertelsmann Stiftung 2020, 2, 15
[168] GSMA n.d.

smartphone connections, and 151 million total mobile connections, with mobile penetration at 49 percent.[169]

According to subscriber data from the Nigerian Communications Commission (NCC), as of July 2020 there were 198,961,361 active mobile lines and 285,259,320 connected mobile lines (Nigeria [2020]).[170] "[T]here is as yet no act that explicitly addresses the subject of digital rights and privacy."

There is "no direct law" that protects data and that pieces of different laws combine to give protection. "There is no overarching federal-level or state-level legislation" for the implementation of the right to privacy.

By section 37 of the Constitution of the Federal Republic of Nigeria, subscribers may view their information in the database system. "[T]he government has conducted mass surveillance of citizens' telecommunications, which has included intercepting private communications."

Government and police may have access to cellphone data by application to the judge: The lawyer noted that police can access personal information that has been provided to cellphone companies with a court order, "but in practice they can access it without one."[171] "It is not commonplace for non-state actors to access personal information, but it is possible" although "the legal framework and self-regulation protect against this."

[169] GSMA 27 Nov. 2018, 2
[170] https://irb-cisr.gc.ca/en/country-information/rir/Pages/index.aspx?doc=458321
[171] *Ibid.*

RPD RULES[172]

Under the
IMMIGRATION AND REFUGEE PROTECTION ACT

Interpretation

1 The following definitions apply in these Rules.

- *Act* means the *Immigration and Refugee Protection Act*. (*Loi*)

- *Basis of Claim Form* means the form in which a claimant gives the information referred to in Schedule 1. (*Formulaire de fondement de la demande d'asile*)

- *contact information* means, with respect to a person,

    - **(a)** the person's name, postal address and telephone number, and their fax number and email address, if any; and

    - **(b)** in the case of counsel for a claimant or protected person, if the counsel is a person referred to in any of paragraphs 91(2)(a) to (c) of the Act, in addition to the information referred to in paragraph (a), the name of the body of

---

[172] Refugee Protection Division Rules, SOR/2012-256

which the counsel is a member and the membership identification number issued to the counsel. (*coordonnées*)

- **Division** means the Refugee Protection Division. (*Section*)

- **officer** means a person designated as an officer by the Minister under subsection 6(1) of the Act. (*agent*)

- **party** means,

    - **(a)** in the case of a claim for refugee protection, the claimant and, if the Minister intervenes in the claim, the Minister; and

    - **(b)** in the case of an application to vacate or to cease refugee protection, the protected person and the Minister. (*partie*)

- **proceeding** includes a conference, an application or a hearing. (*procédure*)

- **registry office** means a business office of the Division. (*greffe*)

- **Regulations** means the <u>Immigration and Refugee Protection Regulations</u>. (*Règlement*)

- **vulnerable person** means a person who has been identified as vulnerable under the *Guideline on Procedures with Respect to Vulnerable Persons Appearing*

Before the IRB issued under paragraph 159(1)(h) of the Act. (*personne vulnérable*)

- **working day** does not include Saturdays, Sundays or other days on which the Board offices are closed. (*jour ouvrable*)

Communicating with the Division

2 All communication with the Division must be directed to the registry office specified by the Division.

Information and Documents to Be Provided
Claims for Refugee Protection

Fixing date, time and location of hearing

- **3 (1)** As soon as a claim for refugee protection is referred to the Division, or as soon as possible before it is deemed to be referred under subsection 100(3) of the Act, an officer must fix a date, time and location for the claimant to attend a hearing on the claim, within the time limits set out in the Regulations, from the dates, times and locations provided by the Division.

Date fixed by officer

(2) Subject to paragraph 3(b), the officer must select the date closest to the last day of the applicable time limit set out in the Regulations, unless the claimant agrees to an earlier date.

Factors

(3) In fixing the date, time and location for the hearing, the officer must consider

- (a) the claimant's preference of location; and

- (b) counsel's availability, if the claimant has retained counsel at the time of referral and the officer has been informed that counsel will be available to attend a hearing on one of the dates provided by the Division.

(4) The officer must

- (a) notify the claimant in writing by way of a notice to appear

  - (i) of the date, time and location of the hearing of the claim; and

  - (ii) of the date, time and location of any special hearing on the abandonment of the claim under subrules 65(2) and (3);

- (b) unless the claimant has provided a completed Basis of Claim Form to the officer in accordance with subsection 99(3.1) of the Act, provide to the claimant the Basis of Claim Form; and

- (c) provide to the claimant information in writing

- **(i)** explaining how and when to provide a Basis of Claim Form and other documents to the Division and to the Minister,

- **(ii)** informing the claimant of the importance of obtaining relevant documentary evidence without delay,

- **(iii)** explaining how the hearing will proceed,

- **(iv)** informing the claimant of the obligation to notify the Division and the Minister of the claimant's contact information and any changes to that information,

- **(v)** informing the claimant that they may, at their own expense, be represented by legal or other counsel, and

- **(vi)** informing the claimant that the claim may be declared abandoned without further notice if the claimant fails to provide the completed Basis of Claim Form or fails to appear at the hearing.

(5) After providing to the claimant the information set out in subrule (4), the officer must without delay provide to the Division

- **(a)** a written statement indicating how and when the information set out in subrule (4) was provided to the claimant;

- **(b)** the completed Basis of Claim Form for a claimant referred to in subsection 99(3.1) of the Act;

- **(c)** a copy of each notice to appear provided to the claimant in accordance with paragraph (4)(a);

- **(d)** the information set out in Schedule 2;

- **(e)** a copy of any identity and travel documents of the claimant that have been seized by the officer;

- **(f)** a copy of the notice of seizure of any seized documents referred to in paragraph (e); and

- **(g)** a copy of any other relevant documents that are in the possession of the officer.

(6) The officer must provide to the claimant a copy of any documents or information that the officer has provided to the Division under paragraphs (5)(d) to (g).

- **4 (1)** The claimant must provide their contact information in writing to the Division and to the Minister.

Time limit

(2) The claimant's contact information must be received by the Division and the Minister no later than 10 days after the day on which the claimant receives the information provided by the officer under subrule 3(4).

Change to contact information

(3) If the claimant's contact information changes, the claimant must without delay provide the changes in writing to the Division and to the Minister.

Information concerning claimant's counsel

(4) A claimant who is represented by counsel must without delay, on retaining counsel, provide the counsel's contact information in writing to the Division and to the Minister and notify them of any limitations on the counsel's retainer. If that information changes, the claimant must without delay provide the changes in writing to the Division and to the Minister.

Declaration — counsel not representing or advising for consideration

5 If a claimant retains counsel who is not a person referred to in any of paragraphs 91(2)(a) to (c) of the Act, both the claimant and their counsel must without delay provide the information and declarations set out in Schedule 3 to the Division in writing.

Basis of Claim Form

Claimant's declarations

- **6 (1)** The claimant must complete a Basis of Claim Form and sign and date the declaration set out in the form stating that

  - o **(a)** the information given by the claimant is complete, true and correct; and

  - o **(b)** the claimant understands that the declaration is of the same force and effect as if made under oath.

Form completed without interpreter

(2) If the claimant completes the Basis of Claim Form without an interpreter's assistance, the claimant must sign and date the declaration set out in the form stating that they can read the language of the form and understand what information is requested.

Interpreter's declaration

(3) If the claimant completes the Basis of Claim Form with an interpreter's assistance, the interpreter must sign and date the declaration in the form stating that

  - o **(a)** they are proficient in the language and dialect, if any, used, and were able to communicate effectively with the claimant;

  - o **(b)** the completed Basis of Claim Form and all attached documents were interpreted to the claimant; and

  - o **(c)** the claimant indicated that the claimant understood what was interpreted.

Providing Basis of Claim Form — inland claim

- **7 (1)** A claimant referred to in subsection 99(3.1) of the Act must provide the original and a copy of the completed Basis of Claim Form to the officer referred to in rule 3.

Providing Basis of Claim Form — port of entry claim

(2) A claimant other than a claimant referred to in subsection 99(3.1) of the Act must provide the original and a copy of the completed Basis of Claim Form to the Division.

Documents to be attached

(3) The claimant must attach to the original and to the copy of the completed Basis of Claim Form a copy of their identity and travel documents, genuine or not, and a copy of any other relevant documents in their possession. The claimant does not have to attach a copy of a document that has been seized by an officer or provided to the Division by an officer.

Documents obtained after providing Basis of Claim Form

(4) If the claimant obtains an identity or travel document after the Division has received the completed Basis of Claim Form, they must provide two copies of the document to the Division without delay.

Providing Basis of Claim Form — port of entry claim

(5) The Basis of Claim Form provided under subrule (2) must be

- **(a)** received by the Division within the time limit set out in the Regulations, and

○ **(b)** provided in any of the following ways:

- **(i)** by hand,

- **(ii)** by courier,

- **(iii)** by fax if the document is no more than 20 pages long, unless the Division consents to receiving more than 20 pages, or

- **(iv)** by email or other electronic means if the Division allows.

Original Basis of Claim Form

(6) A claimant who provides the Basis of Claim Form by fax must provide the original to the Division at the beginning of the hearing.

Application for extension of time

- **8 (1)** A claimant who makes an application for an extension of time to provide the completed Basis of Claim Form must make the application in accordance with rule 50, but the claimant is not required to give evidence in an affidavit or statutory declaration.

Time limit

(2) The application must be received by the Division no later than three working days before the expiry of the time limit set out in the Regulations.

Application for medical reasons

(3) If a claimant makes the application for medical reasons, other than those related to their counsel, they must provide, together with the application, a legible, recently dated medical certificate signed by a qualified medical practitioner whose name and address are printed or stamped on the certificate. A claimant who has provided a copy of the certificate to the Division must provide the original document to the Division without delay.

Content of certificate

(4) The medical certificate must set out the particulars of the medical condition, without specifying the diagnosis, that prevent the claimant from providing the completed Basis of Claim Form in the time limit referred to in paragraph 7(5)(a).

Failure to provide medical certificate

(5) If a claimant fails to provide a medical certificate in accordance with subrules (3) and (4), the claimant must include in their application

- **(a)** particulars of any efforts they made to obtain the required medical certificate, supported by corroborating evidence;

- **(b)** particulars of the medical reasons for the application, supported by corroborating evidence; and

- **(c)** an explanation of how the medical condition prevents them from providing the completed Basis of Claim Form in the time limit referred to in paragraph 7(5)(a).

Providing Basis of Claim Form after extension granted

(6) If an extension of time is granted, the claimant must provide the original and a copy of the completed Basis of Claim Form to the Division in accordance with subrules 7(2) and (3), no later than on the date indicated by the Division and by a means set out in paragraph 7(5)(b).

Changes or additions to Basis of Claim Form

- **9 (1)** To make changes or add any information to the Basis of Claim Form, the claimant must

    - **(a)** provide to the Division the original and a copy of each page of the form to which changes or additions have been made;

    - **(b)** sign and date each new page and underline the changes or additions made; and

    - **(c)** sign and date a declaration stating that

        - **(i)** the information given by the claimant in the Basis of Claim Form, together with the changes and additions, is complete, true and correct, and

        - **(ii)** the claimant understands that the declaration is of the same force and effect as if made under oath.

Time limit

(2) The documents referred to in subrule (1) must be provided to the Division without delay and must be received by it no later than 10 days before the date fixed for the hearing.

Conduct of a Hearing

Standard order of questioning

- **10 (1)** In a hearing of a claim for refugee protection, if the Minister is not a party, any witness, including the claimant, will be questioned first by the Division and then by the claimant's counsel.

  Order of questioning — Minister's intervention on exclusion issue

  (2) In a hearing of a claim for refugee protection, if the Minister is a party and has intervened on an issue of exclusion under subrule 29(3), any witness, including the claimant, will be questioned first by the Minister's counsel, then by the Division and then by the claimant's counsel.

  Order of questioning — Minister's intervention not on exclusion issue

  (3) In a hearing of a claim for refugee protection, if the Minister is a party but has not intervened on an issue of exclusion under subrule 29(3), any witness, including the claimant, will be questioned first by the Division, then by the Minister's counsel and then by the claimant's counsel.

Order of questioning — application to vacate or cease refugee protection

(4) In a hearing into an application to vacate or to cease refugee protection, any witness, including the protected person, is to be questioned first by the Minister's counsel, then by the Division and then by the protected person's counsel.

Variation of order of questioning

(5) The Division must not vary the order of questioning unless there are exceptional circumstances, including that the variation is required to accommodate a vulnerable person.

Limiting questioning of witnesses

(6) The Division may limit the questioning of witnesses, including a claimant or a protected person, taking into account the nature and complexity of the issues and the relevance of the questions.

Oral representations

(7) Representations must be made orally at the end of a hearing unless the Division orders otherwise.

Oral decision and reasons

(8) A Division member must render an oral decision and reasons for the decision at the hearing unless it is not practicable to do so.

Information and Documents to Be Provided (continued)
Documents Establishing Identity and Other Elements of the Claim

Documents

11 The claimant must provide acceptable documents establishing their identity and other elements of the claim. A claimant who does not provide acceptable documents must explain why they did not provide the documents and what steps they took to obtain them.

Application to Vacate or to Cease Refugee Protection

Contact information

12 If an application to vacate or to cease refugee protection is made, the protected person must without delay notify the Division and the Minister in writing of

- **(a)** any change in their contact information; and

- **(b)** their counsel's contact information and any limitations on the counsel's retainer, if represented by counsel, and any changes to that information.

Declaration — counsel not representing or advising for consideration

13 If a protected person retains counsel who is not a person referred to in any of paragraphs 91(2)(a) to (c) of the Act, both the protected person and their counsel must without delay provide the information and declarations set out in Schedule 3 to the Division in writing.

Counsel of Record

Becoming counsel of record

- **14 (1)** Subject to subrule (2), as soon as counsel for a claimant or protected person agrees to a date for a proceeding, or as soon as a person becomes counsel after a date for a proceeding has been fixed, the counsel becomes counsel of record for the claimant or protected person.

  Limitation on counsel's retainer

(2) If a claimant or protected person has notified the Division of a limitation on their counsel's retainer, counsel is counsel of record only to the extent of the services to be provided within the limited retainer. Counsel ceases to be counsel of record as soon as those services are completed.

Request to be removed as counsel of record

- **15 (1)** To be removed as counsel of record, counsel for a claimant or protected person must first provide to the person represented and to the Minister, if the Minister is a party, a copy of a written request to be removed and then provide the written request to the Division, no later than three working days before the date fixed for the next proceeding.

Oral request

(2) If it is not possible for counsel to make the request in accordance with subrule (1), counsel must appear on the date fixed for the proceeding and make the request to be removed orally before the time fixed for the proceeding.

Division's permission required

(3) Counsel remains counsel of record unless the request to be removed is granted.

Removing counsel of record

- **16 (1)** To remove counsel as counsel of record, a claimant or protected person must first provide to counsel and to the Minister, if the Minister is a party, a copy of a written notice that counsel is no longer counsel for the claimant or protected person, as the case may be, and then provide the written notice to the Division.

Ceasing to be counsel of record

(2) Counsel ceases to be counsel of record as soon as the Division receives the notice.

Language of Proceedings

Choice of language — claim for refugee protection

- **17 (1)** A claimant must choose English or French as the language of the proceedings at the time of the referral of their claim for refugee protection to the Division.

Changing language

(2) A claimant may change the language of the proceedings that they chose under subrule (1) by notifying the Division and the Minister in writing. The notice must be received by the Division and the Minister no later than 10 days before the date fixed for the next proceeding.

Choice of language — application to vacate or cease refugee protection

- **18 (1)** The language that is chosen under rule 17 is to be the language of the proceedings in any application made by the Minister to vacate or to cease refugee protection with respect to that claim.

Changing language

(2) A protected person may change the language of the proceedings by notifying the Division and the Minister in writing. The notice must be received by the Division and the Minister no later than 10 days before the date fixed for the next proceeding.

Interpreters

Need for interpreter — claimant

- **19 (1)** If a claimant needs an interpreter for the proceedings, the claimant must notify an officer at the time of the referral of the claim to the Division and specify the language and dialect, if any, to be interpreted.

Changing language of interpretation

(2) A claimant may change the language and dialect, if any, that they specified under subrule (1), or if they had not indicated that an interpreter was needed, they may indicate that they need an interpreter, by notifying the Division in writing and indicating the language and dialect, if any, to be interpreted. The notice must be received by the Division no later than 10 days before the date fixed for the next proceeding.

Need for interpreter — protected person

(3) If a protected person needs an interpreter for the proceedings, the protected person must notify the Division in writing and specify the language and dialect, if any, to be interpreted. The notice must be received by the Division no later than 10 days before the date fixed for the next proceeding.

Need for interpreter — witness

(4) If any party's witness needs an interpreter for the proceedings, the party must notify the Division in writing and specify the language and dialect, if any, to be interpreted. The notice must be received by the Division no later than 10 days before the date fixed for the next proceeding.

Interpreter's oath

(5) The interpreter must take an oath or make a solemn affirmation to interpret accurately.

Designated Representatives

Duty of counsel or officer to notify

- **20 (1)** If counsel for a party or if an officer believes that the Division should designate a representative for the claimant or protected person because the claimant or protected person is under 18 years of age or is unable to appreciate the nature of the proceedings, counsel or the officer must without delay notify the Division in writing.

Exception

(2) Subrule (1) does not apply in the case of a claimant under 18 years of age whose claim is joined with the claim of their parent or legal guardian if the parent or legal guardian is 18 years of age or older.

Content of notice

(3) The notice must include the following information:

- **(a)** whether counsel or the officer is aware of a person in Canada who meets the requirements to be designated as a representative and, if so, the person's contact information;

- **(b)** a copy of any available supporting documents; and

- (c) the reasons why counsel or the officer believes that a representative should be designated.

Requirements for being designated

(4) To be designated as a representative, a person must

- (a) be 18 years of age or older;

- (b) understand the nature of the proceedings;

- (c) be willing and able to act in the best interests of the claimant or protected person; and

- (d) not have interests that conflict with those of the claimant or protected person.

Factors

(5) When determining whether a claimant or protected person is unable to appreciate the nature of the proceedings, the Division must consider any relevant factors, including

- (a) whether the person can understand the reason for the proceeding and can instruct counsel;

- (b) the person's statements and behaviour at the proceeding;

- **(c)** expert evidence, if any, on the person's intellectual or physical faculties, age or mental condition; and

- **(d)** whether the person has had a representative designated for a proceeding in another division of the Board.

Designation applies to all proceedings

(6) The designation of a representative for a person who is under 18 years of age or who is unable to appreciate the nature of the proceedings applies to all subsequent proceedings in the Division with respect to that person unless the Division orders otherwise.

End of designation — person reaches 18 years of age

(7) The designation of a representative for a person who is under 18 years of age ends when the person reaches 18 years of age unless that representative has also been designated because the person is unable to appreciate the nature of the proceedings.

Termination of designation

(8) The Division may terminate a designation if the Division is of the opinion that the representative is no longer required or suitable and may designate a new representative if required.

Designation criteria

(9) Before designating a person as a representative, the Division must

- (a) assess the person's ability to fulfil the responsibilities of a designated representative; and

- (b) ensure that the person has been informed of the responsibilities of a designated representative.

Responsibilities of representative

(10) The responsibilities of a designated representative include

- (a) deciding whether to retain counsel and, if counsel is retained, instructing counsel or assisting the represented person in instructing counsel;

- (b) making decisions regarding the claim or application or assisting the represented person in making those decisions;

- (c) informing the represented person about the various stages and procedures in the processing of their case;

- (d) assisting in gathering evidence to support the represented person's case and in providing evidence and, if necessary, being a witness at the hearing;

- (e) protecting the interests of the represented person and putting forward the best possible case to the Division;

- o **(f)** informing and consulting the represented person to the extent possible when making decisions about the case; and

- o **(g)** filing and perfecting an appeal to the Refugee Appeal Division, if required.

Disclosure of Personal Information

Disclosure of information from another claim

- **21 (1)** Subject to subrule (5), the Division may disclose to a claimant personal and other information that it wants to use from any other claim if the claims involve similar questions of fact or if the information is otherwise relevant to the determination of their claim.

  Notice to another claimant

  (2) If the personal or other information of another claimant has not been made public, the Division must make reasonable efforts to notify the other claimant in writing that

  - o **(a)** it intends to disclose the information to a claimant; and

  - o **(b)** the other claimant may object to that disclosure.

  Request for disclosure

  (3) In order to decide whether to object to the disclosure, the other claimant may make a written request to the Division for personal and other information relating to the claimant. Subject to subrule (5), the Division may disclose only information that is necessary to permit the other claimant to make an informed decision.

Notice to claimant

(4) If the personal or other information of the claimant has not been made public, the Division must make reasonable efforts to notify the claimant in writing that

- **(a)** it intends to disclose the information to the other claimant; and

- **(b)** the claimant may object to that disclosure.

Information not to be disclosed

(5) The Division must not disclose personal or other information unless it is satisfied that

- **(a)** there is not a serious possibility that disclosing the information will endanger the life, liberty or security of any person; or

- **(b)** disclosing the information is not likely to cause an injustice.

Information from joined claims

(6) Personal or other information from a joined claim is not subject to this rule. If claims were once joined but were later separated, only personal or other information that was provided before the separation is not subject to this rule.

Specialized Knowledge

Notice to parties

22 Before using any information or opinion that is within its specialized knowledge, the Division must notify the claimant or protected person and, if the Minister is present at the hearing, the Minister, and give them an opportunity to

- **(a)** make representations on the reliability and use of the information or opinion; and

- **(b)** provide evidence in support of their representations.

Allowing a Claim Without a Hearing

Claim allowed without hearing

23 For the purpose of paragraph 170(f) of the Act, the period during which the Minister must notify the Division of the Minister's intention to intervene is no later than 10 days after the day on which the Minister receives the Basis of Claim Form.

Conferences

Requirement to participate at conference

- **24 (1)** The Division may require the parties to participate at a conference to fix a date for a proceeding or to discuss issues, relevant facts and any other matter to make the proceedings fairer and more efficient.

Information or documents

(2) The Division may require the parties to give any information or provide any document, at or before the conference.

Written record

(3) The Division must make a written record of any decisions and agreements made at the conference.

Notice to Appear

Notice to appear

- **25 (1)** The Division must notify the claimant or protected person and the Minister in writing of the date, time and location of the proceeding.

Notice to appear for hearing

(2) In the case of a hearing on a refugee claim, the notice may be provided by an officer under paragraph 3(4)(a).

Date fixed for hearing

(3) The date fixed for a hearing of a claim or an application to vacate or to cease refugee protection must not be earlier than 20 days after the day on which the parties receive the notice referred to in subrule (1) or (2) unless

  - o **(a)** the hearing has been adjourned or postponed from an earlier date; or

  - o **(b)** the parties consent to an earlier date.

Exclusion, Integrity Issues, Inadmissibility and Ineligibility

Notice to Minister of possible exclusion before hearing

- **26 (1)** If the Division believes, before a hearing begins, that there is a possibility that section E or F of Article 1 of the Refugee Convention applies to the claim, the Division must without delay notify the Minister in writing and provide any relevant information to the Minister.

Notice to Minister of possible exclusion during hearing

(2) If the Division believes, after a hearing begins, that there is a possibility that section E or F of Article 1 of the Refugee Convention applies to the claim and the Division is of the opinion that the Minister's participation may help in the full and proper hearing of the claim, the Division must adjourn the hearing and without delay notify the Minister in writing and provide any relevant information to the Minister.

Disclosure to claimant

(3) The Division must provide to the claimant a copy of any notice or information that the Division provides to the Minister.

Resumption of hearing

(4) The Division must fix a date for the resumption of the hearing that is as soon as practicable,

- **(a)** if the Minister responds to the notice referred to in subrule (2), after receipt of the response from the Minister; or

- **(b)** if the Minister does not respond to that notice, no earlier than 14 days after receipt of the notice by the Minister.

Notice to Minister of possible integrity issues before hearing

- **27 (1)** If the Division believes, before a hearing begins, that there is a possibility that issues relating to the integrity of the Canadian refugee protection system may arise from the claim and the Division is of the opinion that the Minister's participation may help in the full and proper hearing of the claim, the Division must without delay notify the Minister in writing and provide any relevant information to the Minister.

Notice to Minister of possible integrity issues during hearing

(2) If the Division believes, after a hearing begins, that there is a possibility that issues relating to the integrity of the Canadian refugee protection system may arise from the claim and the Division is of the opinion that the Minister's participation may help in the full and proper hearing of the claim, the Division must adjourn the hearing and without delay notify the Minister in writing and provide any relevant information to the Minister.

Integrity issues

(3) For the purpose of this rule, claims in which the possibility that issues relating to the integrity of the Canadian refugee protection system may arise include those in which there is

- **(a)** information that the claim may have been made under a false identity in whole or in part;

- (b) a substantial change to the basis of the claim from that indicated in the Basis of Claim Form first provided to the Division;

- (c) information that, in support of the claim, the claimant submitted documents that may be fraudulent; or

- (d) other information that the claimant may be directly or indirectly misrepresenting or withholding material facts relating to a relevant matter.

Disclosure to claimant

(4) The Division must provide to the claimant a copy of any notice or information that the Division provides to the Minister.

Resumption of hearing

(5) The Division must fix a date for the resumption of the hearing that is as soon as practicable,

- (a) if the Minister responds to the notice referred to in subrule (2), after receipt of the response from the Minister; or

- (b) if the Minister does not respond to that notice, no earlier than 14 days after receipt of the notice by the Minister.

Notice of possible inadmissibility or ineligibility

- **28 (1)** The Division must without delay notify the Minister in writing and provide the Minister with any relevant information if the Division believes that o **(a)** a claimant may be inadmissible on grounds of security, violating human or international rights, serious criminality or organized criminality;

o **(b)** there is an outstanding charge against the claimant for an offence under an Act of Parliament that is punishable by a maximum term of imprisonment of at least 10 years; or

o **(c)** the claimant's claim may be ineligible to be referred under section 101 or paragraph 104(1)(c) or (d) of the Act.

Disclosure to claimant

(2) The Division must provide to the claimant a copy of any notice or information that the Division provides to the Minister.

Continuation of proceeding

(3) If, within 20 days after receipt of the notice referred to in subrule (1), the Minister does not notify the Division that the proceedings are suspended under paragraph 103(1)(a) or (b) of the Act or that the pending proceedings respecting the claim are terminated under section 104 of the Act, the Division may continue with the proceedings.

Intervention by the Minister

Notice of intention to intervene

• **29 (1)** To intervene in a claim, the Minister must provide

- o **(a)** to the claimant, a copy of a notice of the Minister's intention to intervene; and

- o **(b)** to the Division, the original of the notice, together with a written statement indicating how and when a copy was provided to the claimant.

Contents of notice

(2) In the notice, the Minister must state

- o **(a)** the purpose for which the Minister will intervene;

- o **(b)** whether the Minister will intervene in writing only, in person, or both; and

- o **(c)** the Minister's counsel's contact information.

Intervention — exclusion clauses

(3) If the Minister believes that section E or F of Article 1 of the Refugee Convention may apply to the claim, the Minister must also state in the notice the facts and law on which the Minister relies.

Time limit

(4) Documents provided under this rule must be received by their recipients no later than 10 days before the date fixed for a hearing.

Claimant or Protected Person in Custody

Custody

30 The Division may order a person who holds a claimant or protected person in custody to bring the claimant or protected person to a proceeding at a location specified by the Division.

Documents
Form and Language of Documents

Documents prepared by party

- **31 (1)** A document prepared for use by a party in a proceeding must be typewritten, in a type not smaller than 12 point, on one or both sides of 216 mm by 279 mm (8 ½ inches x 11 inches) paper.

Photocopies

(2) Any photocopy provided by a party must be a clear copy of the document photocopied and be on one or both sides of 216 mm by 279 mm (8 ½ inches x 11 inches) paper.

List of documents

(3) If more than one document is provided, the party must provide a list identifying each of the documents.

Consecutively numbered pages

(4) A party must consecutively number each page of all the documents provided as if they were one document.

Language of documents — claimant or protected person

- **32 (1)** All documents used by a claimant or protected person in a proceeding must be in English or French or, if in another language, be provided together with an English or French translation and a declaration signed by the translator.

Language of Minister's documents

(2) All documents used by the Minister in a proceeding must be in the language of the proceeding or be provided together with a translation in the language of the proceeding and a declaration signed by the translator.

Translator's declaration

(3) A translator's declaration must include translator's name, the language and dialect, if any, translated and a statement that the translation is accurate.

Disclosure and Use of Documents

Disclosure of documents by Division

- **33 (1)** Subject to subrule (2), if the Division wants to use a document in a hearing, the Division must provide a copy of the document to each party.

Disclosure of country documentation by Division

(2) The Division may disclose country documentation by providing to the parties a list of those documents or providing information as to where a list of those documents can be found on the Board's website.

Disclosure of documents by party

- **34 (1)** If a party wants to use a document in a hearing, the party must provide a copy of the document to the other party, if any, and to the Division.

Proof that document was provided

(2) The copy of the document provided to the Division must be accompanied by a written statement indicating how and when a copy of that document was provided to the other party, if any.

Time limit

(3) Documents provided under this rule must be received by their recipients no later than

- **(a)** 10 days before the date fixed for the hearing; or

- **(b)** five days before the date fixed for the hearing if the document is provided to respond to another document provided by a party or the Division.

Documents relevant and not duplicate

35 Each document provided by a party for use at a proceeding must

- **(a)** be relevant to the particular proceeding; and

- **(b)** not duplicate other documents provided by a party or by the Division.

Use of undisclosed documents

36 A party who does not provide a document in accordance with rule 34 must not use the document at the hearing unless allowed to do so by the Division. In deciding whether to allow its use, the Division must consider any relevant factors, including

- **(a)** the document's relevance and probative value;

- **(b)** any new evidence the document brings to the hearing; and

- **(c)** whether the party, with reasonable effort, could have provided the document as required by rule 34.

Providing a Document

General provision

37 Rules 38 to 41 apply to any document, including a notice or request in writing.

Providing documents to Division

- **38 (1)** A document to be provided to the Division must be provided to the registry office specified by the Division.

  ### Providing documents to Minister

  (2) A document to be provided to the Minister must be provided to the Minister's counsel.

  ### Providing documents to person other than Minister

  (3) A document to be provided to a person other than the Minister must be provided to the person's counsel if the person has counsel of record. If the person does not have counsel of record, the document must be provided to the person.

How to provide document

39 Unless these Rules provide otherwise, a document may be provided in any of the following ways:

- **(a)** by hand;

- **(b)** by regular mail or registered mail;

- **(c)** by courier;

- **(d)** by fax if the recipient has a fax number and the document is no more than 20 pages long, unless the recipient consents to receiving more than 20 pages; and

- **(e)** by email or other electronic means if the Division allows.

Application if unable to provide document

- **40 (1)** If a party is unable to provide a document in a way required by rule 39, the party may make an application to the Division to be allowed to provide the document in another way or to be excused from providing the document.

Form of application

(2) The application must be made in accordance with rule 50.

Allowing application

(3) The Division must not allow the application unless the party has made reasonable efforts to provide the document to the person to whom the document must be provided.

When document received by Division

- **41 (1)** A document provided to the Division is considered to be received by the Division on the day on which the document is date-stamped by the Division.

When document received by recipient other than Division

(2) A document provided by regular mail other than to the Division is considered to be received seven days after the day on which it was mailed. If the seventh day is not a working day, the document is considered to be received on the next working day.

Extension of time limit — next working day

(3) When the time limit for providing a document ends on a day that is not a working day, the time limit is extended to the next working day.

Original Documents

Original documents

- **42 (1)** A party who has provided a copy of a document to the Division must provide the original document to the Division

  - **(a)** without delay, on the written request of the Division; or

  - **(b)** if the Division does not make a request, no later than at the beginning of the proceeding at which the document will be used.

Documents referred to in paragraph 3(5)(e) or (g)

(2) On the written request of the Division, the Minister must without delay provide to the Division the original of any document referred to in paragraph 3(5)(e) or (g) that is in the possession of an officer.

Additional Documents

Documents after hearing

- **43 (1)** A party who wants to provide a document as evidence after a hearing but before a decision takes effect must make an application to the Division.

Application

(2) The party must attach a copy of the document to the application that must be made in accordance with rule 50, but the party is not required to give evidence in an affidavit or statutory declaration.

Factors

(3) In deciding the application, the Division must consider any relevant factors, including

- **(a)** the document's relevance and probative value;

- **(b)** any new evidence the document brings to the proceedings; and

- **(c)** whether the party, with reasonable effort, could have provided the document as required by rule 34.

Witnesses

Providing witness information

- **44 (1)** If a party wants to call a witness, the party must provide the following witness information in writing to the other party, if any, and to the Division:

- **(a)** the witness's contact information;

- o **(b)** a brief statement of the purpose and substance of the witness's testimony or, in the case of an expert witness, the expert witness's brief signed summary of the testimony to be given;

- o **(c)** the time needed for the witness's testimony;

- o **(d)** the party's relationship to the witness;

- o **(e)** in the case of an expert witness, a description of the expert witness's qualifications; and

- o **(f)** whether the party wants the witness to testify by means of live telecommunication.

Proof witness information provided

(2) The witness information provided to the Division must be accompanied by a written statement indicating how and when it was provided to the other party, if any.

Time limit

(3) Documents provided under this rule must be received by their recipients no later than 10 days before the date fixed for the hearing.

Failure to provide witness information

(4) If a party does not provide the witness information, the witness must not testify at the hearing unless the Division allows them to testify.

Factors

(5) In deciding whether to allow a witness to testify, the Division must consider any relevant factors, including

- **(a)** the relevance and probative value of the proposed testimony; and

- **(b)** the reason why the witness information was not provided.

Requesting summons

- **45 (1)** A party who wants the Division to order a person to testify at a hearing must make a request to the Division for a summons, either orally at a proceeding or in writing.

Factors

(2) In deciding whether to issue a summons, the Division must consider any relevant factors, including

- **(a)** the necessity of the testimony to a full and proper hearing;

- **(b)** the person's ability to give that testimony; and

- **(c)** whether the person has agreed to be summoned as a witness.

Using summons

(3) If a party wants to use a summons, the party must

- (a) provide the summons to the person by hand;

- (b) provide a copy of the summons to the Division, together with a written statement indicating the name of the person who provided the summons and the date, time and place that it was provided by hand; and

- (c) pay or offer to pay the person the applicable witness fees and travel expenses set out in Tariff A of the *Federal Courts Rules*.

Cancelling summons

- **46 (1)** If a person who is summoned to appear as a witness wants the summons cancelled, the person must make an application in writing to the Division.

Application

(2) The person must make the application in accordance with rule 50, but is not required to give evidence in an affidavit or statutory declaration.

Arrest warrant

- **47 (1)** If a person does not obey a summons to appear as a witness, the party who requested the summons may make a request to the Division orally at the hearing, or in writing, to issue a warrant for the person's arrest.

Written request

(2) A party who makes a written request for a warrant must provide supporting evidence by affidavit or statutory declaration.

Requirements for issue of arrest warrant

(3) The Division must not issue a warrant unless

- **(a)** the person was provided the summons by hand or the person is avoiding being provided the summons;

- **(b)** the person was paid or offered the applicable witness fees and travel expenses set out in Tariff A of the *Federal Courts Rules*;

- **(c)** the person did not appear at the hearing as required by the summons; and

- **(d)** the person's testimony is still needed for a full and proper hearing.

Content of warrant

(4) A warrant issued by the Division for the arrest of a person must include directions concerning detention or release.

Excluded witness

48 If the Division excludes a witness from a hearing room, no person may communicate to the witness any evidence given while the witness was excluded unless allowed to do so by the Division or until the witness has finished testifying.

Applications
General

General provision

49 Unless these Rules provide otherwise,

- **(a)** a party who wants the Division to make a decision on any matter in a proceeding, including the procedure to be followed, must make an application to the Division in accordance with rule 50;

- **(b)** a party who wants to respond to the application must respond in accordance with rule 51; and

- **(c)** a party who wants to reply to a response must reply in accordance with rule 52.

How to Make an Application

Written application and time limit

- **50 (1)** Unless these Rules provide otherwise, an application must be made in writing, without delay, and must be received by the Division no later than 10 days before the date fixed for the next proceeding.

Oral application

(2) The Division must not allow a party to make an application orally at a proceeding unless the party, with reasonable effort, could not have made a written application before the proceeding.

Content of application

(3) Unless these Rules provide otherwise, in a written application, the party must

- o **(a)** state the decision the party wants the Division to make;

- o **(b)** give reasons why the Division should make that decision; and

- o **(c)** if there is another party and the views of that party are known, state whether the other party agrees to the application.

Affidavit or statutory declaration

(4) Unless these Rules provide otherwise, any evidence that the party wants the Division to consider with a written application must be given in an affidavit or statutory declaration that accompanies the application.

Providing application to other party and Division

(5) A party who makes a written application must provide

- o **(a)** to the other party, if any, a copy of the application and a copy of any affidavit or statutory declaration; and

- o **(b)** to the Division, the original application and the original of any affidavit or statutory declaration, together with a written statement indicating how and when the party provided a copy to the other party, if any.

How to Respond to a Written Application

Responding to written application

- **51 (1)** A response to a written application must be in writing and

    o **(a)** state the decision the party wants the Division to make; and

    o **(b)** give reasons why the Division should make that decision.

Evidence in written response

(2) Any evidence that the party wants the Division to consider with the written response must be given in an affidavit or statutory declaration that accompanies the response. Unless the Division requires it, an affidavit or statutory declaration is not required if the party who made the application was not required to give evidence in an affidavit or statutory declaration, together with the application.

Providing response

(3) A party who responds to a written application must provide

    o **(a)** to the other party, a copy of the response and a copy of any affidavit or statutory declaration; and

    o **(b)** to the Division, the original response and the original of any affidavit or statutory declaration, together with a written statement indicating how and when the party provided a copy to the other party.

Time limit

(4) Documents provided under subrule (3) must be received by their recipients no later than five days after the date on which the party receives the copy of the application.

How to Reply to a Written Response

Replying to written response

- **52 (1)** A reply to a written response must be in writing.

  Evidence in reply

  (2) Any evidence that the party wants the Division to consider with the written reply must be given in an affidavit or statutory declaration that accompanies the reply. Unless the Division requires it, an affidavit or statutory declaration is not required if the party was not required to give evidence in an affidavit or statutory declaration, together with the application.

  Providing reply

  (3) A party who replies to a written response must provide

  - **(a)** to the other party, a copy of the reply and a copy of any affidavit or statutory declaration; and

  - **(b)** to the Division, the original reply and the original of any affidavit or statutory declaration, together with a written statement indicating how and when the party provided a copy to the other party.

  Time limit

(4) Documents provided under subrule (3) must be received by their recipients no later than three days after the date on which the party receives the copy of the response.

Changing the Location of a Proceeding

Application to change location

- **53 (1)** A party may make an application to the Division to change the location of a proceeding.

  #### Form and content of application

  (2) The party must make the application in accordance with rule 50, but is not required to give evidence in an affidavit or statutory declaration.

  #### Time limit

  (3) Documents provided under this rule must be received by their recipients no later than 20 days before the date fixed for the proceeding.

  #### Factors

  (4) In deciding the application, the Division must consider any relevant factors, including

    o **(a)** whether the party is residing in the location where the party wants the proceeding to be held;

    o **(b)** whether a change of location would allow the proceeding to be full and proper;

    o **(c)** whether a change of location would likely delay the proceeding;

- (d) how a change of location would affect the Division's operation;

- (e) how a change of location would affect the parties;

- (f) whether a change of location is necessary to accommodate a vulnerable person; and

- (g) whether a hearing may be conducted by a means of live telecommunication with the claimant or protected person.

Duty to appear

(5) Unless a party receives a decision from the Division allowing the application, the party must appear for the proceeding at the location fixed and be ready to start or continue the proceeding.

Changing the Date or Time of a Proceeding

Application in writing

- **54 (1)** Subject to subrule (5), an application to change the date or time of a proceeding must be made in accordance with rule 50, but the party is not required to give evidence in an affidavit or statutory declaration.

Time limit and content of application

(2) The application must

- (a) be made without delay;

- o **(b)** be received by the Division no later than three working days before the date fixed for the proceeding, unless the application is made for medical reasons or other emergencies; and

- o **(c)** include at least three dates and times, which are no later than 10 working days after the date originally fixed for the proceeding, on which the party is available to start or continue the proceeding.

Oral application

(3) If it is not possible for the party to make the application in accordance with paragraph (2)(b), the party must appear on the date fixed for the proceeding and make the application orally before the time fixed for the proceeding.

Factors

(4) Subject to subrule (5), the Division must not allow the application unless there are exceptional circumstances, such as

- o **(a)** the change is required to accommodate a vulnerable person; or

- o **(b)** an emergency or other development outside the party's control and the party has acted diligently.

Counsel retained or availability of counsel provided after hearing date fixed

(5) If, at the time the officer fixed the hearing date under subrule 3(1), a claimant did not have counsel or was unable to provide the dates when their counsel would be available to attend a hearing, the claimant may make an application to change the date or time of the hearing. Subject to operational limitations, the Division must allow the application if

- **(a)** the claimant retains counsel no later than five working days after the day on which the hearing date was fixed by the officer;

- **(b)** the counsel retained is not available on the date fixed for the hearing;

- **(c)** the application is made in writing;

- **(d)** the application is made without delay and no later than five working days after the day on which the hearing date was fixed by the officer; and

- **(e)** the claimant provides at least three dates and times when counsel is available, which are within the time limits set out in the Regulations for the hearing of the claim.

Application for medical reasons

(6) If a claimant or protected person makes the application for medical reasons, other than those related to their counsel, they must provide, together with the application, a legible, recently dated medical certificate signed by a qualified medical practitioner whose name and address are printed or stamped on the certificate. A claimant or protected person who has provided a copy of the certificate to the Division must provide the original document to the Division without delay.

Content of certificate

(7) The medical certificate must set out

- **(a)** the particulars of the medical condition, without specifying the diagnosis, that prevent the claimant or protected person from participating in the proceeding on the date fixed for the proceeding; and

- **(b)** the date on which the claimant or protected person is expected to be able to participate in the proceeding.

Failure to provide medical certificate

(8) If a claimant or protected person fails to provide a medical certificate in accordance with subrules (6) and (7), they must include in their application

- **(a)** particulars of any efforts they made to obtain the required medical certificate, supported by corroborating evidence;

- **(b)** particulars of the medical reasons for the application, supported by corroborating evidence; and o **(c)** an explanation of how the medical condition prevents them from participating in the proceeding on the date fixed for the proceeding.

Subsequent application

(9) If the party made a previous application that was denied, the Division must consider the reasons for the denial and must not allow the subsequent application unless there are exceptional circumstances supported by new evidence.

Duty to appear

(10) Unless a party receives a decision from the Division allowing the application, the party must appear for the proceeding at the date and time fixed and be ready to start or continue the proceeding.

New date

(11) If an application for a change to the date or time of a proceeding is allowed, the new date fixed by the Division must be no later than 10 working days after the date originally fixed for the proceeding or as soon as possible after that date.

Joining or Separating Claims or Applications

Claims automatically joined

- **55 (1)** The Division must join the claim of a claimant to a claim made by the claimant's spouse or common-law partner, child, parent, legal guardian, brother, sister, grandchild or grandparent, unless it is not practicable to do so.

Applications joined if claims joined

(2) Applications to vacate or to cease refugee protection are joined if the claims of the protected persons were joined.

Application to join

- **56 (1)** A party may make an application to the Division to join claims or applications to vacate or to cease refugee protection.

Application to separate

(2) A party may make an application to the Division to separate claims or applications to vacate or to cease refugee protection that are joined.

Form of application and providing application

(3) A party who makes an application to join or separate claims or applications to vacate or to cease refugee protection must do so in accordance with rule 50, but the party is not required to give evidence in an affidavit or statutory declaration. The party must also

- **(a)** provide a copy of the application to any person who will be affected by the Division's decision on the application; and

- **(b)** provide to the Division a written statement indicating how and when the copy of the application was provided to any affected person, together with proof that the party provided the copy to that person.

Time limit

(4) Documents provided under this rule must be received by their recipients no later than 20 days before the date fixed for the hearing.

Factors

(5) In deciding the application to join or separate, the Division must consider any relevant factors, including whether

- o **(a)** the claims or applications to vacate or to cease refugee protection involve similar questions of fact or law;

- o **(b)** allowing the application to join or separate would promote the efficient administration of the Division's work; and

- o **(c)** allowing the application to join or separate would likely cause an injustice.

Proceedings Conducted in Public

Minister considered party

- **57 (1)** For the purpose of this rule, the Minister is considered to be a party whether or not the Minister takes part in the proceedings.

Application

(2) A person who makes an application to the Division to have a proceeding conducted in public must do so in writing and in accordance with this rule rather than rule 50.

Oral application

(3) The Division must not allow a person to make an application orally at a proceeding unless the person, with reasonable effort, could not have made a written application before the proceeding.

Content of application

(4) In the application, the person must

- **(a)** state the decision they want the Division to make;

- **(b)** give reasons why the Division should make that decision;

- **(c)** state whether they want the Division to consider the application in public or in the absence of the public;

- **(d)** give reasons why the Division should consider the application in public or in the absence of the public;

- **(e)** if they want the Division to hear the application orally, give reasons why the Division should do so; and

- **(f)** include any evidence that they want the Division to consider in deciding the application.

Providing application

(5) The person must provide the original application together with two copies to the Division. The

Division must provide a copy of the application to the parties.

Response to application

(6) A party may respond to a written application. The response must

- **(a)** state the decision they want the Division to make;

- **(b)** give reasons why the Division should make that decision;

- **(c)** state whether they want the Division to consider the application in public or in the absence of the public;

- **(d)** give reasons why the Division should consider the application in public or in the absence of the public;

- **(e)** if they want the Division to hear the application orally, give reasons why the Division should do so; and

- **(f)** include any evidence that they want the Division to consider in deciding the application.

Providing response

(7) The party must provide a copy of the response to the other party and provide the original response and a copy to the Division, together with a written statement indicating how and when the party provided the copy to the other party.

Providing response to applicant

(8) The Division must provide to the applicant either a copy of the response or a summary of the response referred to in paragraph (12)(a).

Reply to response

(9) An applicant or a party may reply in writing to a written response or a summary of a response.

Providing reply

(10) An applicant or a party who replies to a written response or a summary of a response must provide the original reply and two copies to the Division. The Division must provide a copy of the reply to the parties.

Time limit

(11) An application made under this rule must be received by the Division without delay. The Division must specify the time limit within which a response or reply, if any, is to be provided.

Confidentiality

(12) The Division may take any measures it considers necessary to ensure the confidentiality of the proceeding in respect of the application, including

- **(a)** providing a summary of the response to the applicant instead of a copy; and

- **(b)** if the Division holds a hearing in respect of the application,

- **(i)** excluding the applicant or the applicant and their counsel from the hearing while the party responding to the application provides evidence and makes representations, or

- **(ii)** allowing the presence of the applicant's counsel at the hearing while the party responding to the application provides evidence and makes representations, upon receipt of a written undertaking by counsel not to disclose any evidence or information adduced until a decision is made to hold the hearing in public.

Summary of response

(13) If the Division provides a summary of the response under paragraph (12)(a), or excludes the applicant and their counsel from a hearing in respect of the application under subparagraph (12)(b)(i), the Division must provide a summary of the representations and evidence, if any, that is sufficient to enable the applicant to reply, while ensuring the confidentiality of the proceeding having regard to the factors set out in paragraph 166(b) of the Act.

Notification of decision on application

(14) The Division must notify the applicant and the parties of its decision on the application and provide reasons for the decision.

Observers

Observers

- **58 (1)** An application under rule 57 is not necessary if an observer is a member of the staff of the Board or a representative or agent of the United Nations High Commissioner for Refugees or if the claimant or protected person consents to or requests the presence of an observer other than a representative of the press or other media of communication at the proceeding.

Observers — factor

(2) The Division must allow the attendance of an observer unless, in the opinion of the Division, the observer's attendance is likely to impede the proceeding.

Observers — confidentiality of proceeding

(3) The Division may take any measures that it considers necessary to ensure the confidentiality of the proceeding despite the presence of an observer.

Withdrawal

Abuse of process

- **59 (1)** For the purpose of subsection 168(2) of the Act, withdrawal of a claim or of an application to vacate or to cease refugee protection is an abuse of process if withdrawal would likely have a negative effect on the Division's integrity. If no substantive evidence has been accepted in the hearing, withdrawal is not an abuse of process.

Withdrawal if no substantive evidence accepted

(2) If no substantive evidence has been accepted in the hearing, a party may withdraw the party's claim or the application to vacate or to cease refugee protection by notifying the Division orally at a proceeding or in writing.

Withdrawal if substantive evidence accepted

(3) If substantive evidence has been accepted in the hearing, a party who wants to withdraw the party's claim or the application to vacate or to cease refugee protection must make an application to the Division in accordance with rule 50.

Reinstating a Withdrawn Claim or Application

Application to reinstate withdrawn claim

- **60 (1)** A person may make an application to the Division to reinstate a claim that was made by the person and was withdrawn.

Form and content of application

(2) The person must make the application in accordance with rule 50, include in the application their contact information and, if represented by counsel, their counsel's contact information and any limitations on counsel's retainer, and provide a copy of the application to the Minister.

Factors

(3) The Division must not allow the application unless it is established that there was a failure to observe a principle of natural justice or it is otherwise in the interests of justice to allow the application.

(4) In deciding the application, the Division must consider any relevant factors, including whether the application was made in a timely manner and the justification for any delay.

Subsequent application

(5) If the person made a previous application to reinstate that was denied, the Division must consider the reasons for the denial and must not allow the subsequent application unless there are exceptional circumstances supported by new evidence.

Application to reinstate withdrawn application to vacate or to cease refugee protection

- **61 (1)** The Minister may make an application to the Division to reinstate an application to vacate or to cease refugee protection that was withdrawn.

Form of application

(2) The Minister must make the application in accordance with rule 50.

Factors

(3) The Division must not allow the application unless it is established that there was a failure to observe a principle of natural justice or it is otherwise in the interests of justice to allow the application.

(4) In deciding the application, the Division must consider any relevant factors, including whether the application was made in a timely manner and the justification for any delay.

Subsequent application

(5) If the Minister made a previous application to reinstate that was denied, the Division must consider the reasons for the denial and must not allow the subsequent application unless there are exceptional circumstances supported by new evidence.

Reopening a Claim or Application

Application to reopen claim

- **62 (1)** At any time before the Refugee Appeal Division or the Federal Court has made a final determination in respect of a claim for refugee protection that has been decided or declared abandoned, the claimant or the Minister may make an application to the Division to reopen the claim.

  ### Form of application

  (2) The application must be made in accordance with rule 50 and, for the purpose of paragraph 50(5)(a), the Minister is considered to be a party whether or not the Minister took part in the proceedings.

  ### Contact information

  (3) If a claimant makes the application, they must include in the application their contact information and, if represented by counsel, their counsel's contact information and any limitations on counsel's retainer.

  ### Allegations against counsel

  (4) If it is alleged in the application that the claimant's counsel in the proceedings that are the subject of the application provided inadequate representation,

    - **(a)** the claimant must first provide a copy of the application to the counsel and then provide the original application to the Division, and

- o **(b)** the application provided to the Division must be accompanied by a written statement indicating how and when the copy of the application was provided to the counsel.

Copy of notice of appeal or pending application

(5) The application must be accompanied by a copy of any notice of pending appeal or any pending application for leave to apply for judicial review or any pending application for judicial review.

Factor

(6) The Division must not allow the application unless it is established that there was a failure to observe a principle of natural justice.

(7) In deciding the application, the Division must consider any relevant factors, including

- o **(a)** whether the application was made in a timely manner and the justification for any delay; and

- o **(b)** the reasons why

  - **(i)** a party who had the right of appeal to the Refugee Appeal Division did not appeal, or

- **(ii)** a party did not make an application for leave to apply for judicial review or an application for judicial review.

Subsequent application

(8) If the party made a previous application to reopen that was denied, the Division must consider the reasons for the denial and must not allow the subsequent application unless there are exceptional circumstances supported by new evidence.

Other remedies

(9) If there is a pending appeal to the Refugee Appeal Division or a pending application for leave to apply for judicial review or a pending application for judicial review on the same or similar grounds, the Division must, as soon as is practicable, allow the application to reopen if it is necessary for the timely and efficient processing of a claim, or dismiss the application.

Application to reopen application to vacate or to cease refugee protection

- **63 (1)** At any time before the Federal Court has made a final determination in respect of an application to vacate or to cease refugee protection that has been decided or declared abandoned, the Minister or the protected person may make an application to the Division to reopen the application.

Form of application

(2) The application must be made in accordance with rule 50.

Contact information

(3) If a protected person makes the application, they must include in the application their contact information and, if represented by counsel, their counsel's contact information and any limitations on counsel's retainer, and they must provide a copy of the application to the Minister.

Allegations against counsel

(4) If it is alleged in the application that the protected person's counsel in the proceedings that are the subject of the application to reopen provided inadequate representation,

- **(a)** the protected person must first provide a copy of the application to the counsel and then provide the original application to the Division, and

- **(b)** the application provided to the Division must be accompanied by a written statement indicating how and when the copy of the application was provided to the counsel.

Copy of pending application

(5) The application must be accompanied by a copy of any pending application for leave to apply for judicial review or any pending application for judicial review in respect of the application to vacate or to cease refugee protection.

Factors

(6) The Division must not allow the application unless it is established that there was a failure to observe a principle of natural justice.

(7) In deciding the application, the Division must consider any relevant factors, including

- **(a)** whether the application was made in a timely manner and the justification for any delay; and

- **(b)** if a party did not make an application for leave to apply for judicial review or an application for judicial review, the reasons why an application was not made.

Subsequent application

(8) If the party made a previous application to reopen that was denied, the Division must consider the reasons for the denial and must not allow the subsequent application unless there are exceptional circumstances supported by new evidence.

Other remedies

(9) If there is a pending application for leave to apply for judicial review or a pending application for judicial review on the same or similar grounds, the Division must, as soon as is practicable, allow the application to reopen if it is necessary for the timely and efficient processing of a claim, or dismiss the application.

Applications to Vacate or to Cease Refugee Protection

Form of application

- **64 (1)** An application to vacate or to cease refugee protection made by the Minister must be in writing and made in accordance with this rule.

Content of application

(2) In the application, the Minister must include

- o **(a)** the contact information of the protected person and of their counsel, if any;

- o **(b)** the identification number given by the Department of Citizenship and Immigration to the protected person;

- o **(c)** the date and file number of any Division decision with respect to the protected person;

- o **(d)** in the case of a person whose application for protection was allowed abroad, the person's file number, a copy of the decision and the location of the office;

- o **(e)** the decision that the Minister wants the Division to make; and

- o **(f)** the reasons why the Division should make that decision.

Providing application to protected person and Division

(3) The Minister must provide

- o **(a)** a copy of the application to the protected person; and o   **(b)** the original of the application to the registry office that provided the notice of decision in the claim or to a registry office specified by the Division, together with a written statement indicating how and when a copy was provided to the protected person.

Abandonment

Opportunity to explain

- **65 (1)** In determining whether a claim has been abandoned under subsection 168(1) of the Act, the Division must give the claimant an opportunity to explain why the claim should not be declared abandoned,

      o   **(a)** immediately, if the claimant is present at the proceeding and the Division considers that it is fair to do so; or

      o   **(b)** in any other case, by way of a special hearing.

Special hearing — Basis of Claim Form

(2) The special hearing on the abandonment of the claim for the failure to provide a completed Basis of Claim Form in accordance with paragraph 7(5)(a) must be held no later than five working days after the day on which the completed Basis of Claim Form was due. At the special hearing, the claimant must provide their completed Basis of Claim Form, unless the form has already been provided to the Division.

Special hearing — failure to appear

(3) The special hearing on the abandonment of the claim for the failure to appear for the hearing of the claim must be held no later than five working days after the day originally fixed for the hearing of the claim.

Factors to consider

(4) The Division must consider, in deciding if the claim should be declared abandoned, the explanation given by the claimant and any other relevant factors, including the fact that the claimant is ready to start or continue the proceedings.

Medical reasons

(5) If the claimant's explanation includes medical reasons, other than those related to their counsel, they must provide, together with the explanation, the original of a legible, recently dated medical certificate signed by a qualified medical practitioner whose name and address are printed or stamped on the certificate.

Content of certificate

(6) The medical certificate must set out

- **(a)** the particulars of the medical condition, without specifying the diagnosis, that prevented the claimant from providing the completed Basis of Claim Form on the due date, appearing for the hearing of the claim, or otherwise pursuing their claim, as the case may be; and

- **(b)** the date on which the claimant is expected to be able to pursue their claim.

Failure to provide medical certificate

(7) If a claimant fails to provide a medical certificate in accordance with subrules (5) and (6), the claimant must include in their explanation

- **(a)** particulars of any efforts they made to obtain the required medical certificate, supported by corroborating evidence;

- **(b)** particulars of the medical reasons included in the explanation, supported by corroborating evidence; and

- **(c)** an explanation of how the medical condition prevented them from providing the completed Basis of Claim Form on the due date, appearing for the hearing of the claim or otherwise pursuing their claim, as the case may be.

Start or continue proceedings

(8) If the Division decides not to declare the claim abandoned, other than under subrule (2), it must start or continue the proceedings on the day the decision is made or as soon as possible after that day.

Notice of Constitutional Question

Notice of constitutional question

- **66 (1)** A party who wants to challenge the constitutional validity, applicability or operability of a legislative provision must complete a notice of constitutional question.

Form and content of notice

(2) The party must complete the notice as set out in Form 69 of the *Federal Courts Rules* or any other form that includes

- **(a)** the party's name;

- **(b)** the Division file number;

- **(c)** the date, time and location of the hearing;

- **(d)** the specific legislative provision that is being challenged;

- **(e)** the material facts relied on to support the constitutional challenge; and

- **(f)** a summary of the legal argument to be made in support of the constitutional challenge.

Providing notice

(3) The party must provide

- **(a)** a copy of the notice to the Attorney General of Canada and to the attorney general of each province of Canada, in accordance with section 57 of the *Federal Courts Act*;

- **(b)** a copy of the notice to the Minister;

- o **(c)** a copy of the notice to the other party, if any; and

- o **(d)** the original notice to the Division, together with a written statement indicating how and when the copies of the notice were provided under paragraphs (a) to (c), and proof that they were provided.

Time limit

(4) Documents provided under this rule must be received by their recipients no later than 10 days before the day on which the constitutional argument is made.

Decisions

Notice of decision and reasons

- **67 (1)** When the Division makes a decision, other than an interlocutory decision, it must provide in writing a notice of decision to the claimant or the protected person, as the case may be, and to the Minister.

Written reasons

(2) The Division must provide written reasons for the decision together with the notice of decision

- o **(a)** if written reasons must be provided under paragraph 169(1)(d) of the Act;

- o **(b)** if the Minister was not present when the Division rendered an oral decision and reasons allowing a claim for refugee protection; or

- o **(c)** when the Division makes a decision on an application to vacate or to cease refugee protection.

Request for written reasons

(3) A request under paragraph 169(1)(e) of the Act for written reasons for a decision must be made in writing.

When decision of single member takes effect

- **68 (1)** A decision made by a single Division member allowing or rejecting a claim for refugee protection, on an application to vacate or to cease refugee protection, on the abandonment of a claim or of an application to vacate or to cease refugee protection, or allowing an application to withdraw a claim or to withdraw an application to vacate or to cease refugee protection takes effect

  - o **(a)** if given orally at a hearing, when the member states the decision and gives the reasons; and

  - o **(b)** if made in writing, when the member signs and dates the reasons for the decision.

When decision of three member panel takes effect

(2) A decision made by a panel of three Division members allowing or rejecting a claim for refugee protection, on an application to vacate or to cease refugee protection, on the abandonment of a claim or of an application to vacate or to cease refugee protection, or allowing an application to withdraw a claim or to withdraw an application to vacate or to cease refugee protection takes effect

- o **(a)** if given orally at a hearing, when all the members state their decision and give their reasons; and

- o **(b)** if made in writing, when all the members sign and date their reasons for the decision.

General Provisions

No applicable rule

69 In the absence of a provision in these Rules dealing with a matter raised during the proceedings, the Division may do whatever is necessary to deal with the matter.

Powers of Division

70 The Division may, after giving the parties notice and an opportunity to object,

- **(a)** act on its own initiative, without a party having to make an application or request to the Division;

- **(b)** change a requirement of a rule;

- **(c)** excuse a person from a requirement of a rule; and

- **(d)** extend a time limit, before or after the time limit has expired, or shorten it if the time limit has not expired.

Failure to follow rule

71 Unless proceedings are declared invalid by the Division, a failure to follow any requirement of these Rules does not make the proceedings invalid.

Repeals

72 [Repeal]

73 [Repeal]

Coming into Force

These Rules come into force on the day on which section 26 of the *Balanced Refugee Reform Act* comes into force, but if they are registered after that day, they come into force on the day on which they are registered.

SCHEDULE 1 (Rule 1)

Claimant's Information and Basis of Claim

Item	Information
1	Claimant's name.
2	Claimant's date of birth.
3	Claimant's gender.
4	Claimant's nationality, ethnic or racial group, or tribe.
5	Languages and dialects, if any, that the claimant speaks.
6	Claimant's religion and denomination or sect.
7	Whether the claimant believes that they would experience harm, mistreatment or threats if they returned to their country today. If yes, description of what the claimant expects would happen, including who would harm, mistreat or threaten them and what the claimant believes would be the reasons for it.
8	Whether the claimant or the claimant's family have ever experienced harm, mistreatment or threats in the past. If yes, a description of the harm, mistreatment or threats, including when it occurred, who caused it, what the claimant believes are the reasons for it and whether similarly situated persons have experienced such harm, mistreatment or threats.

Item	Information
9	Whether the claimant sought protection or help from any authority or organization in their country. If not, an explanation of why not. If yes, the authority or organization from which the claimant sought protection or help and a description of what the claimant did and what happened as a result.
10	When the claimant left their country and the reasons for leaving at that time.
11	Whether the claimant moved to another part of their country to seek safety. If not, an explanation of why not. If the claimant moved to another part of their country, the reasons for leaving it and an explanation why the claimant could not live there or in another part of their country today.
12	Whether the claimant moved to another country to seek safety. If yes, details including the name of the country, when the claimant moved there, length of stay and whether the claimant claimed refugee protection there. If the claimant did not claim refugee protection there, an explanation of why not.
13	Whether minors are claiming refugee protection with the claimant. If yes, whether the claimant is the minor's parent and the other parent is in Canada, or whether the claimant is not the minor's parent, or whether the claimant is the minor's parent but the other parent is not in Canada. If the claimant is not the minor's parent or if the claimant is the minor's parent but the other parent is not in Canada, details of any legal documents or written consent allowing the claimant to take care of the minor or travel with

Item	Information
	the minor. If the claimant does not have such documents, an explanation of why not.
14	If a child six years old or younger is claiming refugee protection with the claimant, an explanation of why the claimant believes the child would be at risk of being harmed, mistreated or threatened if returned to their country.
15	Other details the claimant considers important for the refugee protection claim.
16	Country or countries in which the claimant believes they are at risk of serious harm.
17	The country or countries in which the claimant is or has been a citizen, including how and when citizenship was acquired and present status.
18	Name, date of birth, citizenship and place and country of residence of relatives, living or dead, specifically the claimant's spouse, common-law partner, children, parents, brothers and sisters.
19	If the claimant or the claimant's spouse, common-law partner, child, parent, brother or sister has claimed refugee protection or asylum in Canada or in any other country — including at a Canadian office abroad or from the United Nations High Commissioner for Refugees — the details of the claim including the name of the person who made the claim, and the date, location, result of the claim and IRB file number or CIC client ID number, if any.

Item	Information
20	Whether the claimant applied for a visa to enter Canada. If yes, for what type of visa, the date of the application, at which Canadian office the application was made and whether or not it was accepted. If the visa was issued, the date of issue and the duration of the visa. If the application was refused, the date and reasons of refusal.
21	Claimant's contact information.
22	Whether the claimant has counsel and if so, details concerning counsel — including what counsel has been retained to do and counsel's contact information.
23	Claimant's choice of official language for communications with and proceedings before the Board.
24	Whether the claimant needs an interpreter during any proceeding, and the language and dialect, if any, to be interpreted.

SCHEDULE 2 (Paragraph 3(5)(d))

Information To Be Provided About the Claimant by an Officer

Item	Information
1	Name, gender and date of birth.
2	Department of Citizenship and Immigration client identification number.
3	If the claimant is detained, the name and address of the place of detention.
4	Claimant's contact information in Canada, if any.
5	Contact information of any counsel for the claimant.
6	Official language chosen by the claimant as the language of proceedings before the Board.
7	Date the claim was referred or deemed to be referred to the Division.
8	Section of the Act under which the claim is being referred.
9	Officer's decision about the claim's eligibility under section 100 of the Act, if a decision has been made.
10	The country or countries in which the claimant fears persecution, torture, a risk to their life or a risk of cruel and unusual treatment or punishment.

Item	Information
11	Whether the claimant may need a designated representative and the contact information for any proposed designated representative.
12	Whether the claimant needs an interpreter, including a sign language interpreter, during any proceeding, and the language and dialect, if any, to be interpreted.
13	If a claim of the claimant's spouse, common-law partner or any relative has been referred to the Division, the name and Department of Citizenship and Immigration client identification numbers of each of those persons.
14	When and how the officer notified the claimant of the referral of the claim to the Division.
15	Whether the claim was made at a port of entry or inside Canada other than at a port of entry.
16	Any other information gathered by the officer about the claimant that is relevant to the claim.

SCHEDULE 3 (Rules 5 and 13)

Information and Declarations — Counsel Not Representing
or Advising for Consideration

Item	Information
1	IRB Division and file number with respect to the claimant or protected person.
2	Name of counsel who is representing or advising the claimant or protected person and who is not receiving consideration for those services.
3	Name of counsel's firm or organization, if applicable, and counsel's postal address, telephone number, fax number and email address, if any.
4	If applicable, a declaration, signed by the interpreter, that includes the interpreter's name, the language and dialect, if any, interpreted and a statement that the interpretation is accurate.
5	Declaration signed by the claimant or protected person that the counsel who is representing or advising them is not receiving consideration and the information provided in the form is complete, true and correct.
6	Declaration signed by counsel that they are not receiving consideration for representing or advising the claimant or protected person and that the information provided in the form is complete, true and correct.

USEFUL SOURCES

28 Too Many, "Nigeria: The Law and FGM,"
https://www.28toomany.org/static/media/uploads/Law%20
Reports/nigeria_law_report_v1_(june_2018).pdf
https://irb-cisr.gc.ca/en/country-
information/rir/Pages/index.aspx?doc=457956

Amnesty International, ""They Betrayed Us": Women Who
Survived Boko Haram Raped, Starved And Detained In
Nigeria,"
https://www.amnesty.org/en/documents/afr44/8415/2018/
en/
IRB, "Ritual in which a widow must drink the water used to
clean her late husband's corpse; consequences for refusal to
drink this water; whether a widow's refusal is interpreted as
responsibility for her husband's death; state protection,"
https://irb-cisr.gc.ca/en/country-
information/rir/Pages/index.aspx?doc=457660

Bisi Alimi Foundation, "Not dancing to their music: The
Effects of Homophobia, Biphobia and Transphobia on the
lives of LGBT people in Nigeria,"
https://www.bisialimifoundation.org/site/bisialimifoundatio
n/assets/pdf/not-dancing-to-their-music-main-copy.pdf

British Broadcasting Corporation (BBC). 28 August 2014.
"Nigeria Launches National Electronic ID Cards."
http://www.bbc.com/news/world-africa-28970411
Human Rights Watch, "'You Pray For Death': Trafficking of
Women and Girls in Nigeria,"
https://www.hrw.org/sites/default/files/report_pdf/nigeria0
819.pdf

International Lesbian, Gay, Bisexual, Trans and Intersex
Association, "Nigeria. State-Sponsored Homophobia 2019,"

https://ilga.org/downloads/ILGA_State_Sponsored_Homo phobia_2019_light.pdf

IRB, "Domestic violence, including legislation; protection and support services offered to victims (2016-November 2019)," https://irb-cisr.gc.ca/en/country-information/rir/Pages/index.aspx?doc=457962

IRB, "Information on how bisexuality is understood and perceived in Nigeria; whether bisexuality is distinguished from both male and female homosexuality (2014-June 2015)," http://irb-cisr.gc.ca/Eng/ResRec/RirRdi/Pages/index.aspx?doc=45608 9&pls=1

IRB, "National Identity Cards, including implementation of the National Identity Card Policy, requirements and procedures, security features, uses, and whether the card is mandatory," http://irb-cisr.gc.ca/Eng/ResRec/RirRdi/Pages/index.aspx?doc=45615 5&pls=1

IRB, "The death registration process, including the process to obtain a death certificate," http://irb-cisr.gc.ca/Eng/ResRec/RirRdi/Pages/index.aspx?doc=45253 1

IRB, "The Situation of Sexual and Gender Minorities in Nigeria (2014-2018)," https://irb-cisr.gc.ca/en/country-information/research/Pages/situation-gender-minorities-nigeria.aspx

IRB, "Treatment of sexual minorities, including legislation, state protection, and support services; the safety of sexual minorities living in Lagos and Abuja (February 2012-October 2015)," http://irb-cisr.gc.ca/Eng/ResRec/RirRdi/Pages/index.aspx?doc=456219&pls=1

IRB, "Whether lawyers or barristers notarize a statement or swear an affidavit in which an individual admits to being bisexual or homosexual, or to knowing of someone's sexual orientation (2014-October 2016)," http://irb-cisr.gc.ca/Eng/ResRec/RirRdi/Pages/index.aspx?doc=456781

IRB, "Whether parents can refuse female genital mutilation (FGM) of their daughter; state protection available (2016-October 2018)," Whether parents can refuse female genital mutilation (FGM) of their daughter; state protection available (2016-October 2018)

IRB, "Whether Yoruba and Ibo cleansing rituals for women in their thirties include circumcision in the states of Ogun, Niger, Anambra, and Adamawa; whether women who have been accused of killing a family member through witchcraft would be circumcised," http://irb-cisr.gc.ca/Eng/ResRec/RirRdi/Pages/index.aspx?doc=454546&pls=1

Legit.ng. 16 May 2018. Francis Bolaji. "How to Obtain International Driver's License in Nigeria."

Nigeria. 2012. Federal Road Safety Commission. *National Road Traffic Regulations, 2012*.

Nigeria. N.d. National Identity Management Commission. "The Nigerian National Identity Policy."

http://www.nimc.gov.ng/sites/default/files/id_card_policy.pdf

Nigeria, "Same Sex Marriage (Prohibition) Act, 2013," http://www.refworld.org/docid/52f4d9cc4.html

OECD, "Nigeria. Social Institutions and Gender Index 2019," https://www.genderindex.org/wp-content/uploads/files/datasheets/2019/NG.pdf

The Daily Post. 19 September 2015. "Military Discovers Boko Haram Business Centre [Where] Fake National Identity Cards Are Made." http://dailypost.ng/2015/09/19/military-discovers-boko-haram-business-centre-were-fake-national-identity-cards-are-made/

The Guardian. 17 September 2015. "Army Arrests Producers of Fake National ID Cards for Boko Haram Terrorists." http://www.ngrguardiannews.com/2015/09/army-arrests-producers-of-fake-national-id-cards-for-boko-haram-terrorists/

The Initiative for Equal Rights; Vivid Rain, "Social Perception Survey on Lesbian, Gay, Bisexual and Transgender Persons Rights in Nigeria," https://theinitiativeforequalrights.org/wp-content/uploads/2019/08/2019-Social-Perception-Survey.pdf

The Nation. 24 September 2015. "Fake National ID Cards in Circulation, says DHQ." http://thenationonlineng.net/fake-national-id-cards-in-circulation-says-dhq/

UK, "Country Policy and Information Note. Nigeria: Female Genital Mutilation (FGM). Version 2.0.," https://assets.publishing.service.gov.uk/government/uploads/system/uploads/attachment_data/file/825243/Nigeria_-_FGM_-_CPIN_-_v2.0__August_2019_.pdf

UK, "Nigeria: Sexual orientation and gender identity or expression. Version 2.0.," https://assets.publishing.service.gov.uk/government/uploads/system/uploads/attachment_data/file/795440/Nigeria_-_CPIN_-_SOGIE_-_final_version.G__April_2019_.pdf

United Nations (UN). 1968 (amended 2006). United Nations Economic Commission for Europe (UNECE). *Part I: Convention on Road Traffic Done at Vienna on 8 November 1968 (Consolidated Version).*

REFUGEE PREPARATION QUESTIONNAIRE

1. Claimant identification:

Name:
DOB:
Nationality:
Religion/No Religion:
Passport#:
Current Address:
Email:
Tel/Cell:

2. Basis of Claim (BOC):

Your claim may arise in any of the following five (5) grounds (check one):

Political Opinion:
Religion:
Race:
Nationality
Membership in a particular social group/non-state-actors (gangs, tribe, clan, culture, spousal abuse, sexual orientation, etc.):

Do you know your story well? Tell your story in the following format:

Personal identifiers: Who you are, where you come from, and what you are seeking.

Founded fear of persecution: Who wants to harm you (government or non-state-actors; the fear you have if you return to your country or place of your habitual residence. State protection: The government (police, military, etc.) wants to harm you.

Internal flight alternatives: Where you ran to hide from your persecutors within your country or place of habitual residence.

Other factors: Are you a single mother, a woman or a member of the sexual minority? Tell us why you are unable to express yourself.

Is there any need to update, amend or add to your story/narrative new information which recently came to your knowledge?

3. Evidence:

Do you have relevant documents/evidence to support your claim/story? If so, list the documents (add more pages, if required):

If you are submitting affidavits, are the signatures fresh?

Do you have any witness/es to support your claim? If so, list their names and contact details. How do you think they will help you in the hearing? (Add more pages if required).

Narrative details:

Have you mastered/remembered all dates, places, events/time or the order in which events happened?

Do you have a hearing date (date to appear) yet, if so, what is the date?

Have you remembered to submit all the relevant documents and/or amendments to your BOC narrative at least 10 days before the hearing?

Do you hold Green Card from the USA?

Did you pass through the USA to come to Canada, if so, did you claim refugee there, if not, why didn't you claim refugee protection or asylum in USA? (Add more pages if required)

Is the information you provided on your Visa/immigration application the same as you gave in your refugee application? Have you thoroughly checked forms, letters, online account, if any, responses, and etc., to make sure you haven't contradicted yourself in the immigration/refugee application process?

Have you elected or are you thinking of using an interpreter at the hearing, if so, in what language and do you need any help?

Are you comfortable answering questions in shorter sentences?

Are you comfortable understanding Canadian English and accent?

Are you comfortable looking the "Member" (adjudicator or decision-maker or "judge") in the eye when testifying?

Are you reading your story/narrative every day? If not, why?

State of mind:

Do you feel stressed or depressed thinking about your hearing?

Are you are thinking you may be clinically depressed because of what you went through and may need the help of a mental health professional? If so, what help do you need?
Complete disclosure:

To the best of your ability and knowledge, have you told me everything I need to know about your case? If there is anything else you want to tell me, please do (Add more pages if required).

Is there any information or documents that are not in your possession, but you believe they are relevant to support your claim? If so, can you obtain them in good time?

Representation:

Do you know the difference between advocate (your counsel or legal representative) and witness/claimant (you) in the hearing process?

If note. Counsel's role as advocate is to assist you present your case using questions based on your immigration documents and forms, refugee documents and forms, and evidence you provided. An advocate is not allowed to answer questions for you during the hearing. Your role as witness/claimant is to answer the questions truthfully, accurately and credibly by eliciting short, straightforward and pointed answers to my questioning or the Member's questioning of you. Do you have any concerns?

How often do you propose we meet or communicate in order to thoroughly prepare you for the hearing? (Add more pages if required).

4. Basic data:

Height (in centimeters):
Eye color:
Have you used other names before?
Have you used another date of birth before?
Address in Canada (Street number; Street name; City or town;

Province; Postal code):
The date you started living at this address:

Addresses in your country of origin or habitual residence
(Street address; City or town; The date you started living at
this address; The date you stopped living at this address; Did
you live in another country other than this one, if so, provide
its address, the date you stopped living at this address, status
in this other country or territory):

Your telephone number in Canada:

Have you ever had another type of travel document other
than passport?

Family information - marital status (What is your current
marital status? Have you been married or in a common-law
relationship before?):

Children (Do you have any children, including biological,
adopted or step-children, who are not already included in this
claim?):

Parents (Father: Surname/last name; Given name/first name;
Date of birth; Country or territory of birth; Does this parent
live with you? If not, their country or territory; Street address;
City or town; If deceased, give the date of death):

Parents (Mother: Surname/last name; Given name/first
name; Date of birth; Country or territory of birth; Does this
parent live with you? If not, their country or territory; Street
address; City or town; If deceased, give the date of death):

5. Travel to Canada:

How did you arrive in Canada (air, land or sea)?
Where did you enter Canada (point of entry)?

When did you most recently enter Canada?

What is your current status in Canada?

What is the number on your immigration status document (VISA, Visitor's Visa or Study Permit)?

How did you travel? (Date you left; Country or territory you left; City /town; The airport you flew out of; Date you arrived; Country or territory you arrived in; City /town; Province; Airport at which you landed):

6. Education, work, and other activities:

Are you currently studying, or have you ever studied at a post-secondary school?

School or institution name:

Date studies started:

Level of study:

Field of study:

Did you get a degree, diploma, or certificate after completing this program? (If so, country or territory; city or town; province):

Did you serve in any military, militia, civil defense unit, security organization, or police force?

Have you ever held government positions? (If so, date started; date ended):

Work or activity:

Country or territory:

City or town:

Date started:

Date ended:

7. Travel history:

Since the age of 18, have you traveled to a country or territory other than where you live now or where you're a citizen?

Date travel started:

Date travel ended:
Country or territory:
Location:
Purpose of travel:
Status in this country or territory:
Has Canada or any other country ever refused to issue you a visa or permit, denied you entry to the country, or ordered you to leave?

8. Criminality:

Have you ever been convicted of a crime in any country or territory?
Have you ever been arrested or detained in any country or territory?
Have you ever been charged, sought, or wanted for a crime in any country or territory?
Have you ever committed a crime in any country or territory?

9. Admissibility:

Have you supported, been a member of, or been associated with any organizations?
Have you supported, been a member of, or been associated with any organizations that use, used, advocated, or advocates the use of armed struggle or violence to reach political, religious, or social objectives?
Have you been a member of any organization that is or was engaged in criminal activity?
Have you ever witnessed or participated in the ill-treatment of prisoners or civilians, looting, or desecration of religious buildings?
Have you ever used, planned, or advocated the use of armed struggle or violence to reach political, social, or religious objectives?

10: Medical history:

Have you ever had any serious disease or physical or mental disorder?
Do you currently have any infectious diseases?

11. Canada and US Visas:

Are you a lawful permanent resident of the United States (U.S.) with a valid green card (alien registration card)?
Have you held a Canadian visitor visa in the past 10 years?
Do you currently hold a valid U.S. nonimmigrant visa?

12. Refugee/immigration background:

Do you have any family members in Canada?
Did someone help you come to Canada (If yes, name of the person/s and their organization)?

13. Expectations:

What are your expectations, and is there anything more you want me to do to help you better prepare for your hearing (other than meeting in person, when necessary, phone calls or email or other agreed upon forms of correspondence)? (Add more pages if required)

14. Any questions or concerns:

If you have any questions, you could reach counsel/representative at email _____ or phone number _____. If you are dissatisfied with the services and preparations or for any other reasons, please let your counsel/representative know at least 30 days before the hearing/trial.

15. Signed and dated:

ABOUT THE AUTHOR

Best Selling Author, Charles Mwewa (LLB; BA Law; BA Ed; LLM), is a prolific researcher, poet, novelist, lawyer, law professor and Christian apologist and intercessor. Mwewa has written no less than 90 books and counting in every genre and has exhibited his works at prestigious expos like the Ottawa International Book Expo and is the winner of the Coppa Awards for his signature publication, *Zambia: Struggles of My People.*
Mwewa and his family live in the Canadian Capital City of Ottawa.

SELECTED BOOKS BY THIS AUTHOR

1. *ZAMBIA: Struggles of My People (First and Second Editions)*
2. *10 FINANCIAL & WEALTH ATTITUDES TO AVOID*
3. *10 STRATEGIES TO DEFEAT STRESS AND DEPRESSION: Creating an Internal Safeguard against Stress and Depression*
4. *100+ REASONS TO READ BOOKS*
5. *A CASE FOR AFRICA?S LIBERTY: The Synergistic Transformation of Africa and the West into First-World Partnerships*
6. *A PANDEMIC POETRY, COVID-19*
7. *ALLERGIC TO CORRUPTION: The Legacy of President Michael Sata of Zambia*
8. *BOOK ABOUT SOMETHING: On Ultimate Purpose*
9. *CAMPAIGN FOR AFRICA: A Provocative Crusade for the Economic and Humanitarian Decolonization of Africa*
10. *CHAMPIONS: Application of Common Sense and Biblical Motifs to Succeed in Both Worlds*
11. *CORONAVIRUS PRAYERS*
12. *HH IS THE RIGHT MAN FOR ZAMBIA: And Other Acclaimed Articles on Zambia and Africa*
13. *I BOW: 3500 Prayer Lines of Inspiration & Intercession from the Heart: Volume One*
14. *INTERUNIVERSALISM IN A NUTSHELL: For Iranian Refugee Claimants*
15. *LAW & GRACE: An Expository Study in the*

INDEX

discretion, 47

discrimination, 15, 16, 22, 23, 24, 98, 99, 102, 104, 107

disputes, 76

domesticate, 8

dress modestly, 47

drugs, 77

E

eagle. *See* national symbols of Nigeria

educational credentials, 3

Eme Etim Akpan. *See* Nigeria's National Anthem

emotional disposition, 47

employment, 36, 88, 113

evidence, 40, 43, 44, 80

examination, 33, 36

Exclusion Orders. *See* Removal Orders

express entry, 11

F

families. *See* Women

Federal Capital Territory, 62

Female Genital Mutilations (FGM), 2, 21

Financial Action Task Force's (FATF's), 77

fingerprints, 112

flooding, 77

Foreign documents. *See* women

foreign national, 33, 34, 35, 43

Foreign National, 33

foreign travel, 106

former habitual residence, 5, 6, 8, 30, 32, 40

founded fear of persecution, 7, 29, 32

freedom, 47

G

gang. *See* non-state actors

gender. *See* Women

gender-based violence, 100

gender-related persecutions, 2

General Assembly, 20

Generic, 34, 36

Global System for Mobile Communications, 115

God, 216

good faith, 39, 44

green and white. *See* national colors

Greentree Agreement, 76

Gross Domestic Product (GDP), 66

GSM. *See* Global System for Mobile Communications

Guaranty Trust Bank, 112

Gulf of Guinea, 53

H

H&C, 11

habitual residence, 5, 8, 17, 19, 23, 27

health, 107

health workers, 96

healthcare, 96

heroin. *See* drugs

heterosexual. *See* sexual orientation

HIV. *See* HIV/AIDS

HIV self-testing kits. *See* HIV/AIDS

HIV/AIDS, 97

HIV-AIDS, 24, 98, 102

homosexuality, 104

human rights instrument, 15

humanitarian and compassionate considerations, 91

I

ICAC. *See* Integrated Claim Analysis Center

identity documents, 34

IFA, 1, 2, 79, 80, 81, 82, 83, 84, 85, 86, 87, 88, 89, 90, 91, 93, 102

Immigration and Refugee Board, 1, 11, 24, 99

Immigration and Refugee Protection Regulations, 8

Immigration Appeal Division, 12

Immigration Consultants, 12

Immigration Division, 12

immigration documents, 3

immigration forms, 34, 35

Immigration, Refugees and Citizenship Canada, 11

imported weapons, 73

inconsistent, 45

incorrect assumptions. *See* Women

Industries in Nigeria, 67

inherit lands and houses.
See Women

inheritance, 2, 98

In-Land Reporting Centre,
34

inquisitorial process, 47

Integrated Claim Analysis
Center, 35

Interim Federal Health
Program (IFHP), 36

internal flight alternatives.
See IFA

internally displaced
persons (IDPs), 77

Internet-users, 71

interpreter, 46, 48

intersectional approach,
100

Intervene, 35

Interview, 35, 36

Iran, 1, 80

IRB, 11, 12, 33, 38, 47, 80,
81, *See* Immigration and
Refugee Board

IRCC, 11, 35, 36

IRPA, 8, 12, 29, 31, 33, 39

ISIS, 75

Islamic police (HISPA),
105

Islamic state, 75

Ituri, 28

J

Jesus, xiii

John A. Ilechukwu. *See*
Nigeria's National Anthem

Joint Border
Commission with
Cameroon, 76

jurisdiction, 7

K

Kaduna, 96

Katsina, 96

kidnapping, 74

kin, 113

Kingsley Moghalu, 62

L

Labor Party, 62

Lagos, 60, 70, 75, 83, 85,
108

Lake Chad region, 76

law, 213

Law Society, 12

lawyer, 12, 213

Nigeria's currency. *See* Naira

Nigeria's economy, 63

Nigeria's energy sources, 69

Nigeria's external debt, 68

Nigeria's imports-commodities, 67

Nigeria's National Anthem, 63

Nigerian Armed Forces, 72

Nigerian Communications Commission, 70

Nigerian Communications Commission (NCC), 116

no compulsory military conscription, 73

Non-Refoulement, 10

non-state actors, 24

non-State actors, 43, 79, 80

non-verbal, 48

North Kivu, 28

notaries, 3

Notice to Appear, 36, 38

Notice to Appear for a Hearing, 36

Ntem River, 76

O

OAU Convention Governing the Specific Aspects of Refugee Problems in Africa, 28

objective. *See* founded fear of persecution

Ontario Health Insurance Plan or OHIP, 37

opposite sex, 104

organized criminal rings, 43

organized criminality. *See* non-state actors

P

P.O. Aderibigbe. *See* Nigeria's National Anthem

Panel Physician, 36

paramilitary agency. *See* Nigerian Armed Forces

particular social group, 6, 7, 29

passports, 34, *See* immigration documents

Peer Treatment Champions and Mentor Mothers. *See* HIV/AIDS

People's Democratic Party, 53

permanent residence, 11

surveillance, 116

Y

Young children, 39

Young Progressive
Party or YPP, 62

Z

Zambia, 213, 215, 216, 217

Zamfara, 60, 96

Zenith Bank, 112

www.ingramcontent.com/pod-product-compliance
Lightning Source LLC
Chambersburg PA
CBHW061150220326
41599CB00025B/4432